The
Marriage
Ring

$12⁰⁰

The Marriage Ring

'Til Death Do Us Part

Dr. DeWitt Talmage

CHRISTIAN · LITERATURE · CRUSADE
Fort Washington, Pennsylvania 19034

CHRISTIAN LITERATURE CRUSADE

U.S.A.
P.O. Box 1449, Fort Washington, PA 19034

GREAT BRITAIN
51 The Dean, Alresford, Hants., SO24 9BJ

AUSTRALIA
P.O. Box 91, Pennant Hills, N.S.W. 2120

NEW ZEALAND
10 MacArthur Street, Feilding

ISBN 0-87508-321-8

Copyright © 1996
Christian Literature Crusade
Fort Washington, Pennsylvania

This edition 1996

ABOUT THIS BOOK

THE MARRIAGE RING is a historic reprint of Dr. Thomas DeWitt Talmage's work originally published in 1886.

Usually a book 100 years old holds little value for today's readers, except as a glimpse of life then. This volume is different. The message of the book is timeless and vital because although American society has changed greatly, human nature has not. The decline of marriage and the home is even more alarming today than it was 100 years ago, and sin is still the root problem of every culture.

Dr. Talmage preached these chapters as sermons, seeking to spare those considering marriage from making a mistake in the choice of a mate by urging much prayer for God's guidance—since God alone knows the heart of every man and woman.

Dr. Talmage also sought to set forth the responsibilities of each marriage partner, spotlight the problems that arise in any marriage, and stress the need for working these out together, always remembering the vows made to each other and to God.

Today's reader, on the verge of the 21st century, will be amazed to see how accurate Dr. Talmage's forecasts were. There is much here that is both stimulating and challenging. This great preacher-author presents many spiritual insights and principles which the reader can adapt to meet current personal needs.

Because of this, Christian Literature Crusade is re-publishing the seven key chapters of this book in order that the "alarm call" may again be sounded . . . so that men and women will allow God to guide them to His choice of mate, and that they will invite Him to be the head of their home—to His glory and praise.

Mr. Robert L. Van Alstine, a former pastor of Lifegate Baptist Church in Portland, Oregon, and a past director of Baptist Family Agency, Seattle, Washington, served as compiling editor for this revised edition.

He has taken some editorial liberty to help the 20th-century reader span communication gaps, but still sought to maintain the integrity of Talmage's burden and purpose.

Actually, the book has been changed little. A few chapters and paragraphs have been omitted because they failed to add directly to the purpose. To enhance readability, some phraseology has been altered and a number of expressions modernized, but without changing the meaning or lessening the potential impact.

However, where figures are given, they are Dr. Talmage's figures from more than 100 years ago, and the reader should realize that most are much larger today.

Mr. Van Alstine states, "I am convinced that lifetime permanence is God's intent for marriage."

The Editor

THE PROPOSAL

CONTENTS

INTRODUCTION

TO THE CHRISTIAN YOUNG PERSON

THE normal expectation of every young man or woman is marriage. Marriage is ordained of God as the basis for family units and the continuation of mankind. Unfortunately, modern society has turned from this, so you cannot use "society" as your standard. You must base your practices and goals on the Bible.

A lifetime with a marriage partner has great potential for either enhancing or crippling your happiness, Christian testimony, and service. Many Christian young people have sacrificed themselves and their ability to glorify God by marriage outside His will. Often it begins with a lack of dating standards. Who will you date?

Satan and God do not choose the same mate for you. God has one choice; Satan may have many available. It is important then for you to begin early to determine God's choice, and not dabble in Satan's territory. TOO LATE IS TOO LATE!

Yours will not be a popular stand. A casualness toward approaching, beginning, and maintaining marriage is a curse of modern America, and Christianity has not been immune. This was true when this book was originally published more than 100 years ago, but the problems have multiplied many times since then.

If you let peer pressure and prevalent attitudes influence your decisions about whom to date, you are well into one of Satan's time-perfected specialties. YOU SIMPLY CANNOT BE TOO CAREFUL!

Bob Van Alstine, compiler of this book, has learned through years of pastoring and counseling that one of Satan's most successful strategies is having Christian girls attracted to unsaved boys . . . young men who may even pretend to accept Jesus Christ as personal Savior to land the prize.

So be aware: the wrong mate for you may be in your church youth group or Christian school, although these are obviously much safer places to begin looking than in the world.

What are you worth? Do not underrate yourself and your potential for serving and glorifying God . . . or the terrible effect the wrong mate can have on that potential. Your quest for a fit marriage partner may not be easy!

Anticipate entering marriage in GOD'S WILL. Prayerfully reading this book will be a good beginning. It may even cause you to change your attitude and direction if you are now too casual and careless. That hope is one reason this book is available again after so many years. Its message is as old as the Bible and, like the Bible, is never outdated.

When Dr. Talmage wrote this book, sexual involvement outside marriage by Christian young people was neither talked nor written about. Times have changed.

Today's America is terribly different. With its unashamed focus on illicit sexual activity, the very atmosphere seems charged with immorality. As a Christian young person, you should remember that it is impossible for the Holy Spirit of God to be in control of anyone indulging in actions that can (and usually do) lead to sexual indulgences outside marriage.

There is only one way to be sure you will avoid the trap. Dedicate yourself to preserving your chastity. Put yourself in God's care by a sincere commitment to please and glorify Him. Date carefully and prayerfully. Prepare in advance NOT to get into situations which could end in immorality.

Although Chapters 1 and 2 of this book are aimed at men and women separately, you should read both chapters, as well as the entire book.

GOD BLESS YOU AS YOU SEEK THE MATE HE HAS CHOSEN FOR YOU.

CHAPTER ONE

THE CHOICE OF A WIFE

"Is there never a woman among the daughters of thy brethren, or among all my people, that thou goest to take a wife of the uncircumcised Philistines?" (Judges 14:3).

SAMSON, the mighty giant, is here asking consent of his father and mother as to marriage with one whom they thought unfit for him. He was wise in asking their counsel, but not wise in rejecting it. Captivated by her looks, Samson wanted to marry a daughter of one of the hostile nations in the lowlands. She proved to be a deceitful, hypocritical, whining creature who afterward made him a world of trouble until she quit him forever.

In my text his parents rejected his request—saying, in essence: "When there are so many honest and beautiful maidens of your own country, are you so hard put for a lifetime partner that you propose to marry this foreign flirt? Is there such a dearth of lilies in our Israelitish gardens that you must have a Philistine thistle?"

Excuseless was he for such a choice in a land and amid a race celebrated for female loveliness and moral worth—a land and a race of which self-denying Abigail, heroic Deborah, dazzling Miriam, pious Esther, glorious Ruth, and Mary (who hugged to her heart the blessed Lord) were only magnificent specimens. The midnight folded in their hair, the lakes of liquid beauty in their eye, the gracefulness of spring morning in their posture and gait, were only typical of the greater brilliance and glory of their souls.

Likewise, excuseless is any man in our time who makes lifelong alliance with anyone who, because of her disposition, heredity, habits, intellectual imbalance or moral shortcoming, may be said to be "of the Philistines" (the world).

The world never owned such wondrous womanly character, such splendor of womanly manners or such multitudinous instances of wifely, motherly, daughterly, sisterly devotion as it owns today. I have not words to express my admiration for good womanhood! Woman is not only man's equal, but in affectional and emotional nature, which is the best part of us, she is 75% his superior.

Yea, during the last 25 years, through the increased opportunity opened for female education, the women of our country are better educated than the majority of men. If they continue to advance at the current pace, before long the majority of men will have difficulty finding, in the opposite sex, enough ignorance for an appropriate match-up.

If I am under a delusion as to the abundance of good womanhood abroad, judging by my surroundings since the hour I entered life until now, I hope the delusion will last until I depart this life. So, you will understand if I say—in the course of this series of sermons—something that seems severe, I am neither cynical nor disgruntled. I simply seek to perpetuate that which is good, favorable and desirable.

There are in almost every farmhouse in this nation, in almost every home of the great cities, conscientious, self-sacrificing, holy women. There are innumerable Marys sitting at the feet of Christ, innumerable Marthas helping to feed Christ in the persons of his suffering disciples.

There are a thousand capped and spectacled grandmothers Lois bending over Bibles whose precepts they have followed from early girlhood.

Tens of thousands of young women are dawning upon us who are going to bless the world with good and happy homes, who shall eclipse all their predecessors— a fact that will be acknowledged by all men except those who are struck through with moral decay or near fatal insensitivity. More inexcusable than Samson is that man who, amid all this unparalleled munificence of womanhood, marries a fool.

Sadly, some of you are already suffering from such disaster, and to halt others of you from going over the same precipice, I cry out in the words of my text: "Is there never a woman among the daughters of thy brethren, or among all my people, that thou goest to take a wife of the uncircumcised Philistines?"

There are thousands of American pulpits (among them this pulpit) guilty in the fact that in some of the subjects on which men and women need practical advice they have been silent or have beat around the bush in such a fashion as to be ineffectual. About the choice of a lifetime companion—a question in which so much of

time and eternal impact are involved—
what almost universal silence is in the
church, so that there are not ten people
in this church who have heard a discourse
upon this theme. And the first one I myself have ever heard is the one I am
preaching.

We leave to the flippant novel, the spec-
tacular play of the entertainment world or
the jingle of a frivolous poet that which
ought to burden the most tremendous sermon a minister ever preaches from the
day he takes ordination to the day he
meets his God. And so, in this course of
sermons, I am going to hitch up my best
team of horses, set the plow as deep as it
will go and plow straight on from fence to
fence—no matter how many nests may be
ripped up and how many alarmed people
may cry "Whoa!" I will put all the weight
of God's Word on the plow handles and
holler: "Giddap!"

That marriage is the only destination of
the human race is a mistaken idea I want
to correct before I go further. There are
multitudes who will never marry and still
others who are not fit to marry and ought
not. In Great Britain today there are said
to be 948,000 more women than men.
That, I understand, is about the ratio in
America, also. Clearly, millions of women

will never marry.

The supply for matrimony is greater than the demand, the first lesson of which is that women ought to be at least prepared to care for themselves if need be. Then, there are thousands of men who further shorten the potential for matrimony because THEY HAVE NO RIGHT TO MARRY. They have become so corrupt of character that their offer of marriage is an insult to any good woman! Society needs to be corrected on this subject. If a woman who has sacrificed her honor is unfitted for marriage, so is any man who has sacrificed his purity.

What right have you, O masculine beast whose life has been loose, to take under your care the spotlessness of a virgin reared in the sanctity of a respectable home? Should a buzzard court a dove?

First of all—SEEK DIVINE DIRECTION!

About 35 years ago, when Tupper, the English poet, urged men to prayer before they decided upon matrimonial association, people laughed. Many of them have lived to laugh out of the other side of their mouths. The need of Divine direction I argue from the fact that so many men, and so many of them otherwise strong and wise, have wrecked their lives at this juncture.

Witness Samson and this woman of Timnath. Witness Socrates, henpecked by the historical Xantippe. Witness Job, whose wife had nothing to prescribe for his boils but doses of profanity. Witness Ananias, a liar, who might perhaps have been cured by a truthful spouse—yet he married as great a liar as himself, Sapphira.

Witness none other than John Wesley, one of the best men who ever lived, united to one of the most outrageous and scandalous of women, who sat in City Road Chapel making faces at him while he preached. Witness the great art essayist John Ruskin and his marriage wretchedness, and that of the great preacher Frederick W. Robertson.

Witness a thousand hells on earth kindled by unworthy wives—termagants who scold like a winter storm; female spendthrifts who put their earnest and hardworking husbands into bankruptcy; women on drugs like opium (about 400,000 of them in the United States in the 1890's) who will have their drugs though they cause the eternal damnation of the entire household; heartless and overbearing and unreasonable women—

often married to good men. These are the women whose husbands and sons go to the clubhouses and taverns because they can't stand it at home.

On this sea of matrimony, where so many have suffered dreadful shipwreck, am I not right in advising Divine pilotage?

Especially is devout supplication needed because society is so full of artificialities that men are deceived as to whom they are marrying—and no one BUT the Lord knows. After the dressmaker, milliner, jeweler, hair-adjuster and the cosmetic art have completed their work, how is an unsophisticated man to see through it all and make accurate judgment concerning to whom he offers hand and heart?

That makes a lot of disillusioned husbands. They make an honorable marriage contract—but the goods delivered are not like the sample. They were simply swindled. They mistook Jezebel for Longfellow's Evangeline and Lucretia Borgia for Martha Washington.

Aye, as the Indian chief boasted of the scalps he had taken, so there are in society today many coquettes who boast of the masculine hearts they have captured. And these women, though they may live in homelike surroundings, are less honorable than the women of the streets who advertise their infamy. The man envisions heaven and gets hell.

There is so much counterfeit womanhood abroad, it is no wonder some cannot tell the genuine coin from the counterfeit. The effectiveness of the counterfeit is in its resemblance to that which is real. Do you not realize you need Divine guidance when I remind you that mistake is possible in this important affair and, if made, is scripturally irrevocable?

THE WORST POSSIBLE PREDICAMENT IS TO BE UNHAPPILY YOKED TOGETHER!

Surely it must be obvious that it is better not to make the mistake than to attempt hopeless means of correction. But men and women do not reveal all their personal characteristics until after marriage—and how are YOU to avoid committing the fatal blunder?

There is only one being in the universe who can tell you whom to choose and that one is the Lord of Paradise. There is in all the world someone who was made for you as certainly as Eve was made for Adam.

All sorts of mistakes occur because Eve was made out of a rib from Adam's side. No one knows which of his 24 ribs God

used. If you depend entirely upon yourself for the selection of a wife, there are
23 possibilities to one that you will select
the wrong rib. That is gambling of the
worst sort!

Be careful, I implore you—by the fate of
Ahab, whose wife induced him to steal; by
the fate of Macbeth, whose wife pushed
him into massacre; by the fate of James
Ferguson, the philosopher, whose wife entered the room while he was lecturing and
willfully upset his astronomical appara-
tus, so that he turned to the audience
and said: "Ladies and gentlemen, I have
the misfortune to be married to this
woman"; by the fate of Bulwer, the novel-
ist, whose wife's temper was so incompat-
ible that he furnished her with a house
near London and withdrew from her company, leaving her with a dozen dogs she
entertained as pets; by the fate of that
devout and dedicated Christian, John
Milton, who married a termagant after he
was blind—and when someone called her
a rose, the poet said: "I am no judge of
colors but it may be so, for I feel the
thorns daily"; by the fate of an English-
man, whose wife was so determined to
dance upon his grave that he had himself
buried at sea; by the fate of a village minister I knew, whose wife threw a cup of

hot tea across the table into his face, because they differed in some sentiment; by all these (and multitudes more) scenes of disquietude and marital calamity, I implore you to be cautious and prayerful before you enter marriage—which can be as readily a hell as a heaven.

By the bliss of Pliny, whose wife (when her husband was pleading in court) had messengers coming and going to inform her what impression he was making; by the joy of Grotius, whose wife delivered him from prison under the pretense of having books carried out lest they be injurious to his health—she sending her husband out unobserved in one of the bookcases; by the good fortune of Roland, whose wife (talented, heroic, wonderful Madame Roland) translated and composed for him while he was Secretary of the Interior; by the happiness of many a man who has made intelligent choice of a wife capable of being a prime counselor and companion in brightness and in grief, I say: Pray to Almighty God, morning, noon and night, that at the right time and in the right way He will send you a good, honest, loving and sympathetic wife—or that you may be sent to her.

Let me warn you not to let a question of this importance be settled by the celebrated matchmakers in almost every community. Depend upon your own judgment, divinely illumined. But seek the only right answer to this question.

How can any human being, including yourself, who knows neither of the two parties as God knows them and who is ignorant of the future, give such direction as you absolutely REQUIRE in such a crisis? Take the advice of the earthly matchmaker instead of Divine guidance and you may some day be led to use the tragic words of Solomon regarding his home life.

One day his magnificent palace, with its great wide rooms and great wide doors and great wide hall, was too small for him and the loud tongue of a woman who was belaboring him. He retreated to the housetop to get relief from the bombardment. While there he saw a poor man on one corner of the roof with a mattress as his only furniture and the open sky his only covering.

Solomon envies him and cries out: "It is better to dwell in the corner of the housetop than with a brawling woman in a wide house."

And one day during the rainy season the water leaked through the roof of the palace and began to drip into a pan set to catch it. On one side of him, all day long, the water went drip, drip, drip—while on the other side a female companion was quarreling about this and quarreling about that, ceaselessly pelting his ears with bitter words.

Finally, he seized his pen and wrote: "A continual dropping in a very rainy day and a contentious woman are alike."

If Solomon had been as prayerful at the beginning of his life as he was at the close, how much anguish in his home would have been avoided.

BUT HEAR THIS: Prayer about this will amount to nothing unless you pray SOON ENOUGH! Wait until you are fascinated and infatuated and the equilibrium of your soul is disturbed by a magnetic and exquisite personality and then YOU WILL ANSWER YOUR OWN PRAYERS, and you will mistake your infatuation for the very voice of God.

A distinct and essential point to be made is that if you genuinely have a prayerful spirit you will surely avoid all female hypocrites and scoffers at Christianity—and there are a considerable number of them in all communities, although they may not appear to be such. Often they are skillfully contrived counterfeits.

It must be said that the only influence that keeps woman from being considered and treated as a slave is Christianity, since where Christianity is not dominant that is the way she is treated. Yet there are women who will go and hear lecturers malign Christianity and scoff at the most sacred things of the soul.

A woman, though not a Christian, once said to me: "I was persuaded by my husband to go and hear an infidel lecturer once. Going home, I said to him, 'My dear husband, I would not go again even if my refusal should result in our divorcement.'"

She was right. If, after all that Christ and Christianity have done for a woman, she can go again and again and hear such assaults, she is an awful creature and you had better not go near such a reeking lepress. She needs to be cleansed and fumigated before she is fit for decent society—to say nothing of Christian marriage.

What you want, young man, in a wife is not a butterfly of the sunshine, not a giggling nonentity, not a painted doll, not a gossiping gadabout, not a mixture of artificialities which leave you in doubt as to where the fake ends and the woman begins, but an earnest soul—one who cannot only laugh when you laugh but weep when you weep.

There will be wide, deep graves in your path of life and you will both want all the steadying you can get when you come to the verge of them! When your fortune fails, you will want someone to talk to you of the treasures of heaven and not charge you with a bitter "I told you so!"

As far as I can analyze, sincerity and earnestness are the foundation of all worthy wifehood. Get that and you get all! Fail to get that and you get nothing but what you will wish you'd never gotten.

PHYSICAL BEAUTY IS NOT ESSENTIAL.

Don't make the mistake of Samson and Solomon in letting the EYE settle the question in which the coolest of judgment, directed by Divine wisdom, is all-important. He who has no reason for his wifely choice except a pretty face is like a man who would buy a farm because of the flowers by the doorstep.

Beauty can be an asset, and when God gives it He intends it as a womanly benediction. But how uncertain is the tarrying of human beauty. Time will drive its chariot wheels across that bright face, cutting it up, scarring its countenance with deep ruts and gullies.

There is an eternal beauty on the face of some women which a rough and ungallant world may criticize as homeliness, yet they have graces of soul that will keep them attractive for time and glorious through all eternity. How much better such a choice than one whose beauty is but skin-deep.

There are circumstances in which the plainest of wives is a queen of beauty to her husband, whatever her stature or profile. Due to financial panic or betrayal of a business partner a man goes down—and he comes home that evening bearing the tragic burden: "I am ruined. I am in disgrace forever. I care not whether I live or die. The furniture must go, the house must go, we are social outcasts and we'll be cold-shouldered everywhere we go."

After he ceases his tragic tale of woe and she has heard it all in silence, his wife says: "Is that all? Why, you had nothing when we married and you've only come back to where you started. If you think that my happiness and that of our children depends on such trappings you do not know me, though we have been married and lived together these many years. God is not dead and the Bank of Heaven has not suspended payment. If you don't mind, I don't care a cent.

"What little we need of food and raiment the rest of our lives we can get. I don't propose to sit around and mope and groan. Mary, hand me that darning needle. John, light one of the other gas burners. Jimmy, open that register for a little more heat and fetch your father's slippers. I declare! I smell the cake burning."

And while she's busy with the cake, he hears her humming Newton's blessed old hymn about God's provision for tomorrow! Her voice rings clearly on the ending: "Though all the fields should wither, nor flocks nor herds be there; yet God the same abiding, His praise shall tune my voice. For while in Him confiding, I cannot but rejoice."

The husband says, in amazement: "Well, well, you are the greatest woman I ever saw. I thought you might faint dead away when I told you." And as he looks at her, she renders pale the splendor of all the fashion plates of the day and the preceding centuries. And she's HIS!

There is another time when the plainest wife is a queen of beauty to her husband. She has done the work of life. She has reared her children for God and heaven, though not all of them have turned out as they ought. She is dying and her husband stands by. They think over all the years of their companionship—the births, weddings, burials, ups, downs, successes and failures. They talk about God's goodness and His faithfulness.

She has no fear about going. The Lord has sustained her so many years she'll not distrust Him now. The lips of both of them tremble as they say good-bye and encourage each other about an early meeting in "a better world."

The breath is feebler and feebler—then it stops. Are you sure of it? Yes, she's gone.

As one of the neighbors takes the old man gently by the arm and says: "Come, you had better go into the next room and rest," he says: "Wait a moment. I must take one more look at that beautiful face and those beautiful hands. Beautiful! Beautiful!"

My friend, I hope you do not call that death. That is an autumnal sunset. That is a crystalline river pouring into a crystal sea. That is the solo of human life overpowered by hallelujah chorus. That is a queen's coronation. That is heaven! That is the culmination of a marriage made and blessed of God—worth aiming at and striving for.

"A prudent [good, discreet, wise] wife is from the Lord" (Proverbs 19:14b).

CHAPTER TWO

THE CHOICE OF A HUSBAND

"The Lord grant you that ye may find rest, each of you in the house of her husband" (Ruth 1:9).

THIS is the prayer of pious Naomi for Ruth and Orpah, and it is an appropriate prayer now in behalf of unmarried womanhood. Naomi, the good old soul, knew that Satan would take their lives in hand if God did not. So she prays: "The Lord grant you that ye may find rest, each of you in the house of her husband."

In my first sermon, I have given prayerful Christian advice to men in regard to the selection of a wife. Now I give the same prayerful and Christian advice to women in regard to selection of a husband, while in all these sermons saying much that I hope will be appropriate for all ages and all classes.

I applaud the celibacy of a multitude of women who, rather than make unfit selection, have made none at all. It has not been a lack of opportunity for marital contract on their part but their own culture, refinement and scripturally exalted ideas as to what a husband ought to be. They have seen so many women marry silly braggarts, ruffians, drinkers, lifetime incapables, magnificent nothings, or men who before marriage were angelic and afterward diabolic, that they have been alarmed and stood back. They saw so many ships go into the seas of sorrow that they steered clear. Better for a woman to live alone, though she live for a thousand years, than to be married to one of those masculine failures with which society is saturated.

The patron saint of almost every family circle is some such unmarried woman. Among all the families of cousins she moves about, and her coming to each house is as the morning and her going away as the night. In my large circle of kindred—perhaps 20 families in all—it was Aunt Phoebe. Paul gave a letter of introduction to one whom he calls "Phoebe our sister," as she went up from Cenchrea to Rome, commending her for her kindness and Christian service and imploring all to treat her with utmost courtesy. I think my Aunt Phoebe was named after her.

Was there a sickness in any of the households—she was there, ready to sit up and count out the drops of medicine. Was there a marriage—she helped deck out the bride for the altar. Was there a birth—she was there to rejoice at the nativity. Was there a sore bereavement—she was there to console.

She was God's minister of grace and mercy. The children rushed out at her first appearance, crying, "Here's Aunt Phoebe." But for parental interference, they would have pulled her down with their caresses, for she was not very strong and many severe illnesses had given her enough glimpses of the next world to make her heavenly-minded.

Her table was loaded with great books which have fitted whole generations for heaven. "DeWitt," she said to me one day, "twice in my life have I been so overwhelmed with the love of God that I fainted away and could hardly be resuscitated. Don't tell me there is no heaven. I've seen it twice." If you would know how her presence would soothe an anxiety, shift a burden, cheer a sorrow or leave a blessing on every room in the house, ask any of the Talmages.

She had stayed at home, taking care of an invalid father, until the bloom of life had somewhat faded. But she could interest the young folks with some three or four chapters of romance in her personal history. So we knew it was not through lack of opportunity that she was not the queen of one household instead of being a benediction on a whole circle of households.

At about 70 years of age she made her last visit to my house. When she sat in my Philadelphia church I was embarrassed at her presence because I felt that in spiritual matters I had gotten no farther than the *a-b-c*'s, while she had learned the entire alphabet and many years earlier had finished the *x-y-z*'s.

When she departed this life and entered into the next, what a shout there must have been in heaven—from the front door clear up to the back seat of the highest gallery! I saw the other day, in the village cemetery of Somerville, N.J., her resting place. The tombstone bore the words she told me she would like to have inscribed there: "The Morning Cometh."

Had she a mission in the world? Certainly! As much as Florence Nightingale, nurse of the Crimea; Grace Darling, oarswoman of the Longstone Lighthouse; Mary Lyon, teacher of Mount Holyoke; Hannah More, Christian authoress of England; Dorothea Dix, angel of mercy for the insane; Anna Etheridge, among the wounded at Blackburn's Fort; Margaret Breckenridge, at Vicksburg—or thousands of other glorious women like them, who never married.

Appreciate all this, my sister in the Lord, and it will make you deliberate before you rush out of the single state into another—assuring yourself of personal betterment. Deliberate and pray. Pray and deliberate. As I showed you in my former sermon, a man ought to seek Divine guidance in such a crisis. How much more important that you solicit it!

It is easier for a man to find an appropriate wife than for a woman to find a good husband. It is a matter of simple arithmetic, as I showed in my former discourse. Statistics show that women outnumber men by hundreds of thousands. Why this is, we leave others to guess. But it would seem that woman is a favorite with the Lord and therefore He has made more of that kind.

Whatever the reason for it, the fact is certain that she who selects a husband has a smaller number to select from than he who selects a wife. Therefore a woman ought to be especially careful in her choice of lifetime companionship. If a man err in his selection he often will "go off with the boys" for refuge. Such is not usually true of wives, who are more hesitant to dull their sensibilities with alcohol and tobacco.

If a woman makes a bad job of marital selection, the probability is that nothing but a funeral can relieve it—although the curse of divorce is becoming increasingly common. Divorce cases are more interesting public reading than love letters, except for those who write the letters.

Pray God that you will be delivered from irrevocable and tragic mistake! Permit me to share with you some helpful guidelines:

Avoid affiance with a despiser of the Christian religion, whatever else he may have or have not. Marriage to a man who hates Christianity will insure you a life of wretchedness. Oh, how tragically many are the poor souls who can witness to the fact—and how heedless have been hearers of their iliad of woes, while foolishly repeating their marriage blunder.

Such a man will resent your Christian attentions and attendances. He will speak depreciatingly of Christ. Though he may put on a false front in courting you, as soon as the vows are affirmed he will most likely show his true crude self. He will wound all the most sacred feelings of your soul. He will put your home and children under the anathema of the Lord God Almighty, instead of under His blessing.

In addition to the anguish with which he will fill your life there is great danger he will even distract your personal focus upon God, while making your marriage a disaster. If you currently are involved in such an "engagement," your first duty is to break it. My word may have come just in time!

Then, too, do not unite in marriage with a man of bad habits—with the idea of reforming him. How very rarely does such a plan work to any significant degree. Believe me, if now (under the restraint of your godly acquaintance) he will not give up his bad habits, you cannot expect him to do so once your unwise concession to marriage has sanctioned them. Make no mistake—multitudes of wretched women can bear witness to this tragic truth.

It is a well-nigh hopeless pursuit. You

might as well plant a violet in the face of a winter storm with the idea of appeasing it. You might as well run a schooner alongside a burning ship with the idea of saving the ship. The consequence will be that schooner and ship will be destroyed together.

The poorhouses of our nation can tell countless stories of women who married men to reform them. If by 20 or 25 years of age a man has been grasped by intoxicants, he is under such headway that your attempt to stop him will be like running up a railroad track with a wheelbarrow in an attempt to stop an express train. The poisons have kindled their fires in brain and tongue and all the tears of a weeping wife cannot extinguish the flames.

Instead of marrying a man to reform him, let him reform first! Then give him time—to see whether or not his reform is permanent. Let him understand that if he cannot do without his bad habits for two years he must do without you forever. Better yet, never give one who has such terrible baggage dragging him down a second look.

A further caution: avoid union with one supremely selfish or so wound up in himself and his occupation that he has no room for another. You occasionally find a man who spreads himself so widely over the path of life that there is no room for anyone to walk BESIDE him. He is not one blade of a scissors, incomplete without the other blade. Instead, he is a chisel, made to cut his way through life alone. Or a file, full of roughness, made to be drawn abrasively across society. His very disposition is a protest against marriage.

Others are so married to their occupation or profession that the taking of any other bride is a case of bigamy. For example, when Chatterton's essay was not printed because of the death of the Lord Mayor, Chatterton made out the following balance sheet: "Income lost because of unprinted essay, 1 pound 11 shillings and sixpence. Gained in death elegies and essays, 5 pounds and 5 shillings." Putting what he lost opposite what he gained, Chatterton crudely wrote: "Am glad he is dead by 3 pounds 13 shillings and sixpence." Anyone as hopelessly literary as that ought never to marry. His library and laboratory are all the companionship he needs or deserves.

Indeed, some of the mightiest men this world ever saw were single. Cowper, Pope, Newton, Swift, Locke, Walpole, Gibbon,

Hume and Arbuthnot never married. Some of them marriage would have helped! The right kind of wife would have cured Cowper's gloom, given Newton more practicality and been a relief to Locke's overtaxed brain.

A Christian wife might have influenced Hume and Gibbon to belief in Christianity, had she been so unwise as to marry an unbeliever in the first place. But Dean Swift did not deserve a wife, from the way he broke the heart of Jane Waring first, Esther Johnson afterward, then "Vanessa." The great wit of his day, he was outwitted by his own cruelties.

Amid so many possibilities of fatal mistake, am I not right in urging you to seek the unerring wisdom of God—BEFORE you are infatuated?

Because so many marriages ARE fit to be made convinces us they are divinely arranged. Almost every cradle has an affinity toward some other cradle. They may be on opposite sides of the earth, but one child gets out of this cradle and another child gets out of that cradle and with their first steps they start for each other. They may diverge from the straight path, going toward the north, south, east or west. They may fall down, but rise facing one another. They are ever approaching, all through infancy.

The one (all through the years of boyhood) is going to meet the one who is coming (through all the years of girlhood) to meet him. The decision of parents as to what is best concerning them and changes of fortune may for a time change or arrest the two journeys—but on they go. They may never have seen each other. They may never have heard of each other. But the two pilgrims who started at the two cradles are nearing.

After 18, 20, 30 years the two come within sight. At first glance they may even feel a dislike, they may slacken their steps. Yet something the world calls fate and religion calls providence urges them on and on. They come near enough to join hands in social acquaintance. After a while to join hands in friendship—after a while to join hearts.

The delegate from the one cradle comes up the east isle of the church with her father. The delegate from the other cradle comes up the west side. The two long journeys end at the snowdrift of the bridal veil. The two chains made out of many years are forged together by the golden link which the groom puts upon the third finger of her left hand. One on earth, may they be one in heaven.

But there are so many exceptions to the general rule of natural affinity that ONLY those are safe who pray for a heavenly hand to lead them. Because they depend upon themselves and not on God, there are thousands of women every year going to the slaughter. In India women leap on the funeral pyre of a dead husband. We have a worse spectacle than that in America—innumerable women leaping on the funeral pyre of a living husband!

Again, dear young woman, avoid all proposed alliances through newspaper advertisements. Many women, just for fun, have answered such advertisements and have been led on step by step to infinite catastrophe. What a foolish and hazardous escapade. Men who write such advertisements are villains and lepers—without exception. Would you answer them just for FUN?

I will tell you of a safer and healthier fun. Thrust your hand through the cage at a zoo and stroke the back of a cobra from the East Indies. Or put your head in the mouth of a Numidian lion to see if he will bite. These are safer and healthier fun than answering newspaper advertisements for a wife.

My advice is to marry a man who is a fortune in himself. Houses, lands and large inheritance may be well enough, but the wheel of fortune turns so rapidly that through some investment all these may soon be gone. Such are the experiences of life. There are some things, however, that are a perpetual fortune and belong on the potential bride's checklist—good manners, geniality of soul, kindness, intelligence, sympathy, courage, perseverance, industry and wholeheartedness. Marry such a one and you have married a fortune, whether he has an income of $50,000 a year or an income of $500.

A bank is secure according to its capital stock, not to be judged by the deposits from week to week. A man is rich according to his sterling qualities, not according to the vacillation of circumstances which may leave him with a vast amount of resources today and withdraw them from him tomorrow. IF A MAN IS WORTH NOTHING BUT MONEY, HE IS POOR INDEED! Again, history and human experience bear ample proof of such truth.

A man of upright character is rich. He is independent of property or markets. Nothing can buy him out, nothing can sell him out. He may have more money one year than the next, but the better part of his fortune is unchanging. As one man will not become better, another will not become worse.

Yet, do not expect to find a perfect man! If you find one without faults, incapable of making mistakes, never having guessed wrongly, his patience never having been perturbed, immaculate in speech, in temper, in habits—do not marry him. Why? Because you would enact a swindle. What would you, who are imperfect, do with a perfect man?

Of course, there ARE no perfect men. We occasionally find a man who says he never sins. But he lies when he says it. I have had financial dealings with two or three "perfect" men—and they cheated me woefully. Do not, therefore, frustrate yourself unmercifully looking for an immaculate husband. You'll never find him.

But do not become cynical on this subject. God has a great multitude of grand men who know how to make a home happy. When they come to be husbands they display nobility of nature and a self-sacrificing spirit that surprise even the wife. The greatness of a man is measured in his goodness.

These are the men who cheerfully sit in dark and dingy business offices, 10' x 12', in summertime—hard at work while wives and daughters are away at spas and hot springs. These are the men who, never having had much education themselves, will have sons going off to college and university. These are the men who work themselves to death and leave significant estates and generous life insurance provision for their families. Good men!

There are husbands and fathers here in our midst who would die for their households. This is what makes an army of defense of a country fight more desperately than an army of conquest. It is not so much the sentiment of a flag as it is a wife and children at home that turns enthusiasm into protective fury. The world has such men by the millions, and the small men that infest our communities are guilty of hindering women from appreciating the glory of true manhood.

I was reading of a bridal reception. The young man had brought home the choice of his heart, in her elaborate and exquisite apparel. As she stood in the drawing room amid the happy group, the young man's eyes filled with tears of joy as he considered her actually being HIS.

Years passed by and they stood in the same parlor on another festal occasion. She wore the same dress, for business had not opened as brightly to the young husband as he had hoped. He had never been able to purchase for her another dress. Her face was not as bright and smooth as it had been years before and a careworn look had made its signature upon her countenance.

As he looked at her, he saw the difference between this occasion and the former. He went over to where she sat and said: "You remember the time when we were here before? You have the same dress on. Circumstances have changed, but you look to me far more beautiful than you did then."

There is such a thing as conjugal fidelity and many of you know it in your own homes and are greatly blessed thereby. But please be reminded, young woman, you must start with that GOOD man!

But after all the good advice we may give you, we come back to the golden pillar from which we started—the tremendous truth that no one but God can guide you to safety in this matter of marriage—that may decide your happiness in two worlds, this and the next. So, my sister, I put your case where Naomi put that of Ruth and Orpah when she said: "The Lord grant you that ye may find rest, each of you in the house of your husband."

Imagine the hour for which you pledged your troth has arrived. There is much merrymaking among your young friends, but there is an undertone of sadness in all the house. Your choice may have been the gladdest and best and the joy of all the relatives. But when a young eaglet is about to leave the old nest and is preparing to put out into sunshine and storm for itself, it feels its wings tremble.

So she has a good cry before leaving home and at the marriage father and mother always cry (or feel like it). If you think it is easy to give up a daughter in marriage, though it be with the brightest of prospects, you will think differently when the day comes for you to share that experience.

To have all along watched her from infancy to girlhood, from girlhood to womanhood, studious of her welfare, her slightest illness an anxiety, her presence in your home an ever-increasing joy—and then to have her go away to some other home. . . . Aye, all the redolence of orange blossoms, all the chime of marriage bells, all the rolling of wedding march and the hilarious congratulations of your friends cannot make you forget that you are suffering irreparable loss.

It is a part of parenting. But you know it is all right and you have a personal remembrance of an embarkation just like it 25 or 30 years ago, in which you were one of the departing parties. Suppressing as far as possible your sadness and turning over to God your sincere concern, you say it simply: "Good-bye!"

I hope that you, the departing daughter, will not forget to often write home. For, whatever betide you, the old folks will never lose their interest in your welfare. Make visits to them as often and stay as long as you can, for there will be changes at the old place after a while. Every time you go home you will find more gray hairs on your father's head and more wrinkles in mother's brow. After a while, you will notice that the elastic step has given way to decrepitude.

Some day one of the two pillars of your early home will fall. Then the other pillar will fall. It will be a genuine comfort if, when they are gone, you can feel that while you are faithful in your new home you never forgot your old home and the best friends you ever had—those to whom you are more indebted than you can ever be to anyone else except to God. I mean your father and mother.

Alexander Pope put it into effective rhythm when he said:

> *"Me let the tender office long engage*
> *To rock the cradle of reposing age;*
> *With lenient arts extend a mother's breath,*
> *Make languor smile and smooth the bed*
> *of death;*
> *Explore the thought, explain the asking eye,*
> *And keep awhile one parent from the sky."*

And now I commend all this precious and splendid young womanhood before me today to the God "who setteth the solitary in families." May seeds planted today bear good fruit in due season.

CHAPTER THREE

DUTIES OF HUSBANDS TO WIVES

"And Isaac went out to meditate in the field at the eventide; and he lifted up his eyes, and saw, and, behold, the camels were coming" (Genesis 24:63).

A BRIDAL pageant on the backs of camels! The camel is called the Ship of the Desert. Its rolling, swinging motion in the distance is suggestive of a sea vessel rising and falling with the billows. Though awkward looking, how imposing these creatures are as they move along, whether in ancient or modern times, sometimes carrying 400 or 4,000 travelers from Bagdad to Aleppo or from Bassora to Damascus.

In my text there comes a caravan. We notice the noiseless step of the broad foot, the velocity of motion, the gay caparison of saddle and girth, the awning sheltering the riders from the sun and the hilarity of the mounted passengers. We cry out: "Who are they?"

Well, Isaac has been praying for a wife, and it is time he had one, for he is 40 years of age. His servant, directed by the Lord, has made a selection of Rebekah. With her companions and maidens she is on her way to her new home, carrying with her the blessing of all her friends.

Isaac is in the fields meditating upon his proposed passage from celibacy to monogamy. He sees a speck against the sky, then groups of people. After a while he finds that the grandest earthly blessing that ever comes to a man is approaching with this elaborate caravan.

The drivers command the camels to kneel. Putting foot on the neck of the stooping beast, the bride dismounts and greets the man who was as worthy of her as she was worthy of him. "Then Isaac brought her into his mother Sarah's tent. . . . And she became his wife, and he loved her."

In this discourse, already having spoken on the choices of lifetime companions, I take it for granted, O man, your marriage was divinely arranged and that the camels have arrived from the right direction and at the right time, bringing the one intended for you—a Rebekah and not a Jezebel.

I proceed now to tell you how you ought to treat your wife. My ambition is to tell you more plain truth than you have ever heard in any three-quarters of an hour in your life.

First of all, I charge you to realize your responsibility in having taken her from the custody and care and homestead in which she has been sheltered. What courage you must have had and what confidence in yourself to say to her, practically: "I will be to you more than your father and mother and more than all the friends you ever had or ever can have. Give up everything and take me. I feel competent to see you through life in safety.

"You are an immortal being, but I am competent to defend you and make you happy. However bright and comfortable a home you have now, and though in one of the rooms is the armchair in which you were rocked and in the attic is the cradle in which you were hushed and the trundle-bed in which you slept—though in the living room are the father and mother who have gotten wrinkle-faced and stoop-shouldered and dim-eyed in taking care of you . . . yet, you will do better to come with me."

I am amazed that any one of us ever had the sublimity of impudence to ask such a transfer!

But that is the boldness of every man who proffers marriage. He says: "I will navigate you through the storms, the cyclones, the fogs of a lifetime. I will run our ship clear of rocks and icebergs. I have no experience and I have no sea chart, but 'All Aboard!' for the voyage of a lifetime. I admit there have been 10,000 shipwrecks on this very route, but don't hesitate. Tut, tut—there now, don't cry! Brides must not cry at the wedding."

In response to this, the woman (by her action) practically says: "I have but one life to live and I entrust it all to you. My arm is weak, but I depend on the strength of yours. I don't know much of the world, but I rely on your wisdom. I put my body, my mind, my soul, my time in your keeping.

"I make no reserve. Even my name I resign and take yours, though mine is a name that suggests all that is honorable in my father, all that was good in my mother, and all that was pleasant in my brothers and sisters. I start with you on a journey which shall never part except at the edge of your grave or mine.

"Ruth, the Moabitess, made no more thorough self-abnegation than I make when I take her tremendous words, the pathos of which many centuries have not cooled: 'Entreat me not to leave thee, or to return from following after thee: for wither thou goest, I will go, and where thou lodgest, I will lodge; thy people shall be my people, and thy God my God. Where thou diest, will I die, and there will I be buried: the Lord do so to me, and more also, if ought but death part thee and me.'

"Side by side in life. Side by side in the burying-ground. Side by side in heaven. Before God and man and with my immortal soul in the oath, I swear eternal fidelity."

Now, my brother, how ought you to treat her?

Unless you are an infinite ingrate, you will treat her supremely well. You will treat her better than anyone in the universe except your God. Her name will have more music in it than all Chopin or Bach or Rheinberger composed. Her eyes, swollen with three weeks of night-watching over a child with fever, will be to you beautiful as a May morning.

After the last rose petal has dropped out of her cheek, after the last feather of the raven's wing has fallen from her hair, after across her forehead and under her eyes and across her face are as many wrinkles as there are graves over which she has wept, you will be able to truthfully say, in the words of Solomon's Song: "Behold, thou art fair, my love! Behold, thou art fair!"

And perhaps she might respond appropriatively, in the words that no one but the matchless Robert Burns could ever have found pen and ink or heart or brain to write:

> *"John Anderson, my jo, John,*
> *We clamb the hill thegither;*
> *And mony a canty day, John,*
> *We've had wi' ane anither.*
>
> *Now we maun totter down, John,*
> *But hand in hand we'll go;*
> *And sleep thegither at the foot,*
> *John Anderson, my jo."*

If anyone assail her good name you will have hard work to control your temper, and if you should strike him down the sin will not be unpardonable. By as complete a surrender as the universe ever saw, except that of the Son of God for your salvation and mine, she has a first mortgage on you body, mind and soul—and the mortgage is foreclosed. You do not more thoroughly own your two eyes or your two hands than she owns you. And you've agreed to the contract.

The longer the journey Rebekah makes and the greater the risks of her expedition on the back of the camel, the more thoroughly is Isaac bound to be kind, indulgent and worthy.

Now, be honest and pay those debts. You promised to make her happy. Are you making her happy? I trust you are an honest man in other things and feel the importance of keeping a contract. If you have induced her into the marriage relationship under certain pledges of kindness and valuable attention found in your marriage vows and have failed to fulfill your word, you deserve to have a suit brought against you for getting goods under false pretenses. Then you ought to pay large damages.

Review, now, all the fine, beautiful, complimentary, gracious and glorious things you promised her before marriage. Reflect on whether you have kept your faith. Are you being honest? Were you honest then? Do you now say: "Oh, that was all sentimentalism and romance and a joke," or "They all talk that way"?

Well, then, let that plan be tried on YOU! Suppose I am selling land. I fill your mind with roseate speculation. I tell you a city is already laid out on the large farm I propose to sell you and that a new railroad will run close by and have a depot for easy transportation of the crops; that eight or ten capitalists are going to put up fine residences close by.

The climate is delicious and the ground is fertile. Every dollar planted will grow a bush bearing $10 or $20. My speech glows with enthusiasm until you rush off with me to an attorney to have the deed drawn, the money paid down and the bargain completed.

You can hardly sleep nights because of the wonders you are about to experience. You give up your home in the East, you bid good-bye to old neighbors and you take the train. After many days' journey you arrive at a quiet depot from which you take a wagon 30 miles into the wilderness. You reach your new place.

You see a man seated on a wet log in a swamp, shivering with an attack of chills and fever. You ask him who he is. He says: "I am a real estate agent, having in charge the property around here." You ask him where the new depot is. He tells you it has not yet been built, but no doubt will be if the company gets its bill for the track through the next legislature.

You ask him where the new city is laid out. He says, through chattering teeth: "If you will wait until this chill is off, I will show it to you on the map I have in my pocket." You ask him where the capitalists are going to build their fine houses. He says: "Somewhere along those lowlands, out there by the woods—after the water has been drained off."

That night you sleep in the hut of the real estate agent, and though you pray for everyone else, you do not pray for me.

Being more fortunate than many men who go out in such circumstances, you have money enough to get back. You come to me. Out of breath in your indignation, you say: "You have swindled me out of everything. What do you mean, deceiving me about that Western property?" "Oh," I reply, "that was sentimentalism and romance and a joke. That's the way they all talk."

The very thought of such a charade makes the hair of indignation stand up on the back of your neck.

But more excusable would I be in such deception than you who by glow of words and personal magnetism induced a womanly soul into surroundings you have taken no care to make comfortable or attractive. So she exchanged her father's house for the dismal swamp of married experience—treeless, flowerless, shelterless, comfortless and ungodly. I would not be half so much to blame in cheating you out of a farm as you are in cheating a woman out of the happiness of a lifetime!

Take me seriously, now. Honestly compare the promises you made and see whether or not you have kept them.

Some of you spent every evening of the week with your betrothed before marriage. Since then you spend every evening away, except when you have some sickness and the doctor says you must not go out. You used to fill your conversation with interjections of adulation. Now you think it sounds silly to praise the one who ought to be more attractive to you as the years go by and life grows in severity of struggle and becomes more sacred by the baptism of tears—tears over losses, tears over graves.

Compare the way some of you used to come home in the evening when you were attempting to capture her affections and the way you come into the house in the evening now. Then what politeness, what distillation of smiles, what graciousness—sweet as the peach orchard in blossom week.

Now some of you come in and put your hat on the rack, scowl and say: "Lost money today!" You sit down at the table and criticize the way the food is cooked. You shove back before the others are done eating and snatch up the evening paper—oblivious of what has been going on in that home all day.

The children are in awe before the domestic autocrat. Bubbling over with fun, yet they must be quiet; with healthful curiosity, yet they must ask no questions.

The wife has had enough annoyances in nursery, parlor and kitchen to fill her nerves with nettles and spikes. As you have provided money for food and wardrobe, you feel you have done all that is required of you. Toward the good cheer, intelligent improvement and moral entertainment of that home, which at the longest can last but a few years, you are doing nothing.

You seem to have no realization of the fact that soon these children will be grown up or in their graves. They will be far removed from your influence and the wife will soon end her earthly mission. The house will be occupied by others and you, yourself, will be gone.

Gentlemen, fulfill your contracts!

Christian marriage is an affectional arrangement. In heathen lands a man wins his wife by achievements. In some countries wives are bought by payment of so many dollars, as so many cattle or sheep. In one country the man gets on a horse and rides down to where a group of women are standing, seizes one of them by the hair and lifts her, struggling and resisting, on his horse. If her brothers and friends do not overtake them before they get to the jungle, she is his lawful wife.

In another land the masculine candidate for marriage is beaten by the club of the one he would make his bride. If he cries out under the pounding, he is rejected. If he receives the blows uncomplainingly, she is his by right.

Endurance, bravery and skill decide the marriage in barbarous lands, but Christian marriage is a voluntary bargain in which you promise protection, support, companionship and love.

Businessmen have in their fireproof safes a file of papers containing their contracts. Sometimes they take them out and read them over to see what the party of the first part and the party of the second part really bound themselves to do. Different ministers of religion have their own peculiar forms of marriage ceremony, but if you have forgotten what you contracted at the altar of wedlock you had better buy or borrow an Episcopal prayer book. It contains the substance of all intelligent marriage ceremonies when it says:

"I take thee to be my wedded wife, to have and to hold from this day forward, for better or for worse, for richer or for poorer, in sickness and in health, to love and to cherish till death do us part, according to God's holy ordinance, and thereto I pledge thee my troth."

Would it not be a good idea to have that printed in tract form and widely distributed?

The fact is, many men are more kind to other men's wives than to their own. They will let the wife carry a heavy coal scuttle upstairs and will at one bound clear the width of a parlor to pick up some other lady's handkerchief.

And there is an evil which I have seen under the sun. It is common among men, namely husbands—flirtation. The attention they ought to put upon their own wives they bestow upon others. They smile on them coyly, archly, with a manner that seems to say: "I wish I were free from that old drudge at home. What an improvement you would be in my present surroundings." Bouquets are sent, accidental meetings take place, and late at night the man comes home whistling and hilarious and wonders why his wife is jealous.

There are thousands of men who, while not positively immoral, need radical correction of their habits in this direction. It is meanness immeasurable for a man by his behavior to seem to say to his wife: "You can't help yourself. I will go where I please and admire whom I please—and I defy your criticism."

Why, if you are such a man, did you not have that put into the marriage bond? Why did you not have it understood before you were pronounced husband and wife that she should have only a part of the dividend of your affection? That when, as time rolled on and the cares of life had erased some of the bright lines from her face and given unwieldiness to her form, you would have reserved the right to pay obeisance to cheeks more rosy and a figure more lithe and more agile? As you demanded the last ounce of patience and endurance on her part, you could have tapped the marriage document and said: "It's in the bond!"

If this modern Rebekah had understood beforehand where she was alighting, she would have ordered the camel drivers to turn the caravan backward toward Padan-aram.

Flirtation has its origin either in dishonesty or licentiousness. The married man who indulges in it is either a fraud or a no-good. However high up in society such a one may be, and however sought after, I would not give a dime for the virtue of either the masculine or feminine flirt.

The most worthy thing for thousands of married men to do is to go home and apologize for past neglects and brighten up their old love. Take up the family Bible and read the record of the wedding day. Open the drawer of relics and the box inside the drawer containing the trinkets of your dead child. Take up that pack of yellowed letters that were written during your courting days. Rehearse the scenes of joy and sorrow in which you have been mingled as one.

Put all these things as fuel on the altar and by a coal of sacred fire rekindle the extinguished light. It was a blast from hell that blew it out and a gale from heaven can fan it into a blaze.

Ye broken marriage vows, speak out!

Take your wife into all your plans, your successes, your defeats, your ambitions. Tell her everything. Walk arm-in-arm with her into places of amusement, up the rugged way of life, down through dark ravine. When one trembles on the way, let the other be re-enforcement. In no case pass yourself off as a single man practising gallantries. Do not, after you are 50 years of age, try to look young-mannish to the ladies.

Interfere not with your wife's religious nature. Put her not in that awful dilemma in which so many Christian wives are placed by their husbands, who ask them to go to places or do things which compel them to decide between loyalty to God and loyalty to husband. Rather than ask her to compromise her Christian character, encourage her to be more and more a

Christian. There will be times in your life when you will want the help of all her Christian resources. Certainly, when you remember how much influence your mother had over you, you do not want the mother of your own children to set a less holy example!

It pleases me greatly to hear the unconverted and worldly husband say about his wife, with no idea it will get to her ears: "There is the most godly woman alive. Her goodness is a perpetual rebuke to my waywardness. Nothing on earth could ever induce her to do a wrong thing. I hope the children will take after her instead of after me. If there is any heaven at all, I am sure she will go there."

Do you not think it would be a wise and a safe thing for you to join her on the road to heaven? You think you have a happy home now, but what a home you would have if you both were saved! What a new sacredness it would give to your marital relations and what a new light it would throw on the foreheads of your children. In sickness, what a comfort! In reverses of fortune, what a wealth! In death, what a triumph!

God meant you to be the high priest of your household!

Go home today, take the Bible on your lap and gather all your family around you. Those not living will hear of it in a flash and (as ministering spirits) will hover— father, mother and children gone, plus all your celestial kindred.

Then, kneel down. If you cannot think of a prayer to offer, I will give you a prayer: "Lord God, I surrender myself, my beloved wife and these dear children. For our blessed Lord's sake, forgive all the past and help us for all the future. We have lived together here, may we live together forever. Amen and amen!"

Dear me, what a stir that would make among your best friends on earth and in heaven!

Joseph the Second, emperor of the Holy Roman Empire, was kind and so philanthropic he excited the unbounded love of most of his subjects. He abolished slavery, established toleration, and lived in the happiness of his people.

One day, while on his way to Ostend to declare it a free port and while at the head of a great procession, he saw a dejected woman at the door of her cottage. The emperor dismounted and asked the cause of her grief. She said her husband had gone to Ostend to see the emperor and had declined to take her with him. As he was an alien, he could not understand her loyal enthusiasm and that it was the one great desire of her life to see the ruler whose kindness, goodness and greatness had won her unspeakable admiration. Her disappointment in not being able to go and see him was well nigh unbearable.

The Emperor Joseph took from his pocket a box decorated with diamonds surrounding a picture of himself and presented it to her. When the picture revealed to whom she was talking, she knelt in reverence and clapped her hands in gladness before him.

The emperor took the name of her husband and the probable place where he might be found at Ostend. He then had him imprisoned for the three days of the emperor's visit. Returning home, the husband found his wife had seen the emperor, while he had not.

In many families of this earth the wife, through the converting grace of God, has seen "the King in His beauty" and He has conferred upon her the pearl of great price—while the husband is "an alien from the covenant of promise, without God and without hope in this world," imprisoned in worldliness and sin. Oh, that they might go arm-in-arm this day and see Him who is not only greater and lovelier than any Joseph of earthly dominion, but "high over all, in earth and air and sky."

His touch is life. His voice is music. His smile is heaven.

CHAPTER FOUR

DUTIES OF WIVES TO HUSBANDS

*"Now the name of the man was Nabal; and
the name of his wife Abigail; and she was
a woman of good understanding, and of a
beautiful countenance. . ." (1 Samuel 25:3).*

THE ground in Carmel is white, not
with fallen snow but with the wool
from the backs of 3,000 sheep—for they
are being sheared. I hear grinding of iron
blades together and bleating of the flocks,
held between the knees of the shearers
while the clipping goes on. I hear the rus-
tic laughter of the workmen.

Nabal and his wife, Abigail, preside over
this homestead. David, the warrior, sends
a delegation to apply for aid at this prosperous time of sheep-shearing. Nabal de-
clines his request, for the rest of the verse
says Nabal is "churlish and evil in his
doings."

Revenge is the cry! Yonder over the rocks come David and 400 angry men, with one stroke to demolish Nabal, his sheepfolds and vineyards. The regiment marches in double-quick step, stones of the mountain loosen and roll down as the soldiers strike them with their swift and vengeful feet. The cry of the commandery is, "Forward! Forward!"

Abigail, to save her husband and his property, hastens to the foot of the hill. She is armed not with sword or spear, but with her own beauty and self-sacrifice. When David sees her kneeling at the base of the rock, he cries to his storm of men: "Halt! Halt!" The caverns echo it: "Halt! Halt!"

Abigail is the conqueress. One woman in the right mightier than 400 men in the wrong! By her prowess and tact she has saved her husband and home and put before all ages an illustrious specimen of what a wife can do if she be godly, prudent, self-sacrificing, vigilant, devoted to the interests of her husband—and attractive.

As I took to the responsibility of telling husbands how they ought to treat their wives—and though I noticed that some of the men squirmed a little in their pews, they endured it well—I now take the responsibility of telling how wives ought to treat their husbands.

I hope your domestic alliance was so happily formed that while married life may have revealed in him some frailties that you did not suspect, it has also displayed excellences that more than overbalance them. I suppose if I could look into the hearts of 100 wives here present and ask them where is the kindest and best man they know of, and they dared speak out, 99 of the 100 would say: "At the other end of this pew."

Though sometimes you may have snapped each other up a little quick, I hope most of you are as well paired as a couple of whom I read. The wife said to her husband: "I have made up my mind to be submissive, notwithstanding all the misfortunes that have come upon us." They had lost their children, he had lost his health (hence the income of his profession) and the wife had temporarily lost her eyesight.

"Yes," said the husband, "we ought to be submissive. Let me see what we have to submit to. First, we have a home; we can submit to that. Then, we have each other; we can submit to that. We have food and raiment; we can submit to that. We have a great many friends; we can submit to that. We have a Heavenly Father to provide for us. . . ." "Stop!" cried the wife, "I will talk no more about submission."

I hope, my sister, you have married a man as Christian and well-balanced as that. But even if you were worsted in the marriage bargain, you cannot be worse off than this Abigail of my text.

The very evening of her heroic achievement at the foot of the mountain, where she captured an entire regiment with genial and strategic behavior, she returned home and found her husband so drunk she could not tell him the story. She had to postpone it until the next day.

So, my sister, I do not want you to keep saying within yourself as I proceed: "That is the way to treat a PERFECT husband." You are to remember that no wife was ever worse swindled than this Abigail. At the other end of her table sat a mean, selfish, snarling, contemptible sot. If she could do so well for such an accursed creature, how ought you to do with that princely, splendid—though imperfect— man with whom you walk the path of life?

First, I counsel the wife to remember in

what a severe and terrific battle of life her husband is engaged.

Whether in professional, commercial, artistic or mechanical life, your husband from morning to night is in a battle, if not a war. It is a wonder he has any nerves or patience left. To get a living in this next to the last decade of the 19th century is a struggle, at best. If he comes home and sits down preoccupied, you ought to at least be gracious. If he does not feel like going out that night for a walk or entertainment, remember he has been out all day.

You say he ought to leave his annoyances at his place of business and come home cheery. Ideally, that would be so. But if a man has been betrayed by a business partner or a customer has jockeyed him out of a large bill of goods or someone has called him a liar, if everything has gone wrong from morning to night, he must have great genius at forgetfulness if he does not bring some of the perplexity home with him. When you tell him he ought to leave it all at the store or bank or shop, you might as well tell a storm on the Atlantic to stay out there and not touch the coast or ripple the harbor.

Remember, he is not overworking so

much for himself as he is overworking for you and the children. It is the effect of his success or defeat on the homestead that causes him agitation.

Most men after 45 years of age live not for themselves, but for their families. They begin to ask themselves anxiously the question: "If I should give out, what would become of the folks at home? Would my children ever get their education? Would my wife have to go out into the world to earn bread for herself and our little ones? My eyesight troubles me; what if my eyes should fail? My head gets dizzy; what if I should drop under apoplexy?" The high pressure of business life, mechanical life and agriculture life is HOME pressure.

Some time ago a large London firm decided if any one of its clerks married on a salary less than 150 pounds (that is, $750) a year, he should be discharged—the supposition being that the temptation might be too great for him to misappropriate goods or funds. The large majority of families in America live by utmost dint of economy. They serve the infamous twins, Scratch and Scrape. To be honest and yet meet one's family expenses is the appalling question that turns the life of tens of thousands of men into martyrdom.

Let the wife of the overburdened and exhausted husband remember this: Do not nag him about this and nag him about that and say you might as well have no husband, when the fact is he is dying by inches that the home may be kept up.

I charge the wife, also, to keep herself as attractive after marriage as she was before marriage. Often, the reason a man ceases to lavish love upon his wife, frankly speaking, is because the wife ceases to be lovely. In many cases, what elaboration of enhancement of appearance before marriage and what recklessness of appearance after!

The most disgusting thing on earth is a slatternly woman. I mean a woman who never combs her hair until she goes out and looks a fright until someone calls. That a man married to one of these creatures stays at home as little as possible is no wonder! It is a wonder such a man does not go on a whaling voyage of three years—and in a leaky ship.

Costly wardrobe is not required. But, O woman, if you are not willing (by all the ingenuity that personal refinement can effect) to make yourself attractive to your husband, you ought not to complain if he seeks in other society those humanly pleasant surroundings you deny him. The same is true of maintaining a tidy home with whatever you have to work with, whether he seems to appreciate it or not— but especially if you are blessed with a man whose nature thrives on some semblance of neatness and order.

Again, I charge you: Never talk to others about the frailties of your husband. Some people have a way, in banter, of elaborately describing to others the shortcomings or unhappy eccentricities of a husband or wife. Ah, the world will find out soon enough the defects of your companion. No need of your advertising them. Better imitate those women who, having made mistakes in marrying, seek the more to hide imperfections.

We must admit there are rare cases where a wife cannot live longer with a husband. His cruelties and outrages are the precursor to separation. But until that day comes keep the awful secret to yourself—keep it from every being in the universe except God, to whom you do well to tell your trouble.

Trouble, yes, but for only a few years at most. Then you can go up on the other side of the grave and say: "O Lord, I kept the marital secret. Thou knowest how well

I kept it and I thank Thee that the release has come at last. Give me some place where I can sit down and rest a while from the horrors of an embruted earthly alliance before I begin the full raptures of heaven." Orders will ultimately be sent to the usher angels, saying: "Take this Abigail right up to the softest seat in the best room in the palace and let twenty of the brightest angels wait on her for the next thousand years."

Furthermore, I charge you: Let there be no outside interference in your marriage. Neither neighbor nor confidential friend, nor brother nor sister, nor father nor mother has a right to come in here. The married gossip will come around and by the hour tell you how she manages her husband. Tell her plainly that if she will attend to the affairs of her household you will attend to yours.

What damage some people do with their tongues. The natural formation indicates the tongue is a dangerous thing by the fact it is shut in—first by a barricade of teeth and then by the door of the lips. Would that the teeth were more often clenched and the lips closed. One insidious talker can keep an entire neighborhood badly stirred up.

The Apostle Peter excoriated these busybodies in other people's matters and the Apostle Paul, in his letter to the Thessalonians and to Timothy, gives them a sharp and purposeful dig. The good housewife will be on the lookout for them, never return their calls and treat them with coldest frigidity. They'll seek more receptive ears.

In your married relations you do not need any advice. If you and your husband have not skill enough to get along well alone, with all the advice you can import you will not do better. What you want for your craft on this voyage is plenty of sea room, and if one of these steam-tugs of marital advice comes puffing alongside, with one stroke cut the hawser and go your way. If your own mother seeks to steer your married ship, remind her gently that God has ordained that you leave her arms and cleave submissively to your husband—a definite and purposeful, though not callous, action.

I charge you, also, to make yourself the intelligent companion of your husband. What with floods of newspapers and books, there is no excuse for the wife's ignorance—either about the present or the past. If you have no more than half an hour every day to yourself, you may become conversant in useful knowledge and awareness.

Let the merchant's wife read up on mercantile questions and the mechanic's wife on his work, the professional's wife on that which pertains to his particular profession—be it legal, medical, theological or whatever. It is very discouraging for a man, after having been amid active minds all day, to find his wife without information or opinion on anything.

If the wife knows nothing about what is going on in the world, after the tea hour has passed and the husband has read the newspaper he is likely to develop the habit of venturing out from the home. In nine cases out of ten, when a man does not stay at home in the evening (unless positive duty calls him) it is because there is nothing to stay home for. He would rather talk with his wife than anyone else, but she must be able to carry on balanced conversation.

At risk of repeating myself, my sister, I charge you in every way to make your home attractive! I have not enough practical knowledge about house adornment to know just what makes the difference. But here is an opulent house, containing all wealth of bric-à-brac, of musical instruments, of painting and of upholstery—yet there is in it a chill like Nova Zembla. Another home, with one-twentieth part of the outlay, small supply of art and cheapest piano purchasable, conveys (as you enter it) to body, mind and soul a glow of welcome, satisfaction and happy domesticity. Every wife should study the holy art of making the most comfort and brightness out of the means she is afforded.

At the siege of Argos, Pyrrhus was killed by the tile of a roof thrown by a woman. Abimelech was slain by a stone that a woman threw from the Tower of Thebez. Earl Montfort was destroyed by a rock discharged at him by a woman from the walls of Toulouse. But without any weapon save that of her cold, cheerless household arrangement any wife may slay all the attractions of a home circle.

A wife and mother in prosperous circumstances and greatly admired was giving the major portion of her time and energies to social life. The husband spent his evenings away. The son, 15 years of age, got the same habit and there was the probability that the other children (as they got old enough) would take the same turn.

The wife realized she had better save her husband and son. Interesting and stirring games were introduced into the house. The mother studied up interesting things to narrate to her children.

One morning, the son said: "Father, you ought to have been home last night. We had a GRAND time! Such jolly games and such interesting stories." This went on from night to night. After a while, the husband stayed in to see what was going on. He finally got attracted and added something of his own to the evening entertainment. The result was the wife and mother saved husband, son and self.

Was that not an enterprise on equal plane with that of Abigail, at the foot of the mountain, who arrested 400 armed warriors?

Do not, my sister, be dizzied and disturbed by the talk of those who think the home circle too insignificant for a woman's career and who want to get you out on platforms and into conspicuous enterprises!

There are women who have a special outside mission—and do not dare to interpret me as derisive of their important mission. But my opinion is the woman who can re-enforce her husband in the work of life and rear her children for usefulness is doing more for God and the race and her own happiness than if she spoke on every great platform and headed a hundred great enterprises.

My mother never made a missionary speech in her life and at a missionary meeting I doubt she could have gotten enough courage to vote yes or no. But she reared her son, John, who has been preaching the gospel and translating religious literature in China for some 40 years. Was that not a better thing to do?

Compare such an individual with one of these frivolous married coquettes of the modern drawing-room. Her heaven is an opera box on opening night, the Ten Commandments an unwelcome inconvenience. She uses innumerable artificialities to create an artificial personal appearance. One is compelled to discuss her character and wonder whether the line between a decent and indecent life is, like the equator, an imaginary line.

WHAT THE WORLD WANTS NOW IS ABOUT 50,000 OLD-FASHIONED MOTHERS—WOMEN WHO SHALL REALIZE THAT THE HIGHEST, GRANDEST INSTITUTION ON EARTH IS THE HOME!

It is not necessary they should have the

same old-time manners of the country farmhouse or wear the old-fashioned cap, spectacles and apron their glorified ancestors wore. My focus is upon the old spirit which began with the Hannahs and the mother Lois and the Abigails of Scripture days and was demonstrated in the homesteads where some of us were reared, though the old house long ago was pulled down and its occupants scattered.

While there are more good and faithful wives and mothers now than there ever were, society has got a wrong twist on this subject and there are influences abroad that would make women believe their chief sphere is outside instead of inside the home.

In many households, children, instead of being considered a blessing, are a nuisance. Hence, infanticide and prenatal murder are so common physicians are crying out in horror. It is time the pulpits joined with the medical profession in echoing and re-echoing the thunder of Mount Sinai, which says "Thou shalt not kill"; and the Book of Revelation, which says "All murderers shall have their place in the lake which burneth with fire and brimstone."

And the abortionist will as certainly go straight to hell as the man or woman who destroys a life 40 years old. The wildest, loudest shriek of the Judgment Day will be given at the overthrow of those who moved in high and respected circles of earthly society, yet decreed by their own act (as far as they could personally effect it) extermination of the advancing generations, abetted in the horrid crime by a lot of infernal quacks with which modern medicine is infested.

On that day, the Judge, with thunderbolt of justice, shall smite the nations into silence and the trial of all the patricides, matricides, fratricides, sororicides, mariticides, uxorcides, regicides, deicides and infanticides of the earth shall proceed. None of my hearers or readers can say they knew not what they were doing. Almighty God, arrest this evil that is overshadowing this century!

I charge you, my sister, that you take your husband along with you to heaven. Of course, this implies that you, yourself, are a Christian. I must take that for granted for the most part. It cannot be possible that after what Christianity has done for woman and after taking the infinitely responsible position you have assumed as a mother you should be antagonistic to Christ.

There is a scriptural sense in which we men are the head of the household, but in some realistic ways it is a pleasant delusion. To whom do the children first go when they have trouble? When there is a sore finger to be bound up or one of the first teeth needs to be removed to make way for one that is crowding it out, to whom does the child go? For whom do children cry out at night when they are frightened by a bad dream? Aye—to whom does the husband go when he hurts?

We, the men, are heads of the household more in name than in fact and it is your business, O wives, to take your husbands with you to glory and to see that the household is prepared for heaven.

You can do it! Of course, God's almighty grace alone can convert him. But often the wife is His instrument. More often than not, it is the wife who first responds to the Holy Spirit's urgings to salvation. Some wives keep their husbands out of heaven—others garner them for it.

If your religion, O wife, is simply the joke of the household; if you would rather go to the theater than the prayer meeting; if you can beat all the neighborhood at card games; if your husband never sees you kneel at the bedside in prayer; if the only thing that reminds your family of your spirituality is that on communion Sunday you get home late for dinner, you will not be able to lead your husband to heaven—and may not be headed there yourself.

But I assume your religion is genuine and the husband realizes there is in your soul a divine principle. Perhaps he sees your quicker temper modified and senses your uncommon tolerance of his imperfections. Your holy example is but one of the oars. The other is prayer. You must pull on both with consecrated effort.

Oh, but you say he belongs to a worldly club or he does not believe a word of the Bible. Or he is a drunkard and very loose in his habits. What you tell me shows you do not understand that while you are at one end of the prayer the omnipotent God is at the other end.

I have no doubt there will be great conventions called in heaven for celebrative purposes; and when in some celestial assemblage the saints shall be telling what brought them to God, I believe that ten thousand times ten thousand voices will say: "My wife!"

I put beside each other two testimonies

of men concerning their wives and let you see the contrast:

An aged man was asked the reason for his salvation. With tearful emotion, he said; "My wife was brought to God some years before myself. I persecuted and abused her because of her religion. She, however, returned nothing but kindness, constantly maintaining an anxiety to promote my comfort and happiness. It was her amiable conduct when suffering ill-treatment from me that first sent the arrows of conviction to my soul."

The other testimony was from a dying man: "Harriet, I am a lost man. You opposed our family worship and my secret prayer. You drew me away into temptation and to neglect every religious duty. I believe my fate is sealed. Harriet, you are a major cause of my everlasting ruin."

As once you stood in the village or city church or in your father's house (perhaps under a wedding bell of flowers), today stand up, husband and wife—beneath the cross of the pardoning Redeemer—while I proclaim the banns of an eternal marriage. Join your right hands.

I pronounce you one forever. What God hath joined together, let neither life nor death nor time nor eternity put asunder.

Witness men and angels, all worlds, all ages! The circle is an emblem of eternity and that is the shape of the marriage ring.

CHAPTER FIVE

MOTHERHOOD

"Moreover his mother made him a little coat, and brought it to him from year to year, when she came up with her husband to offer the yearly sacrifice" (1 Samuel 2:19).

THE story of Abigail and David is very apt to discourage a woman's soul. She says within herself: "It is impossible that I can ever achieve any such grandeur of character and I don't mean to try"—as though a child should refuse to play the eight notes because he cannot execute a "William Tell."

This Hannah of the text differs much from Abigail. She was an ordinary woman with ordinary intellectual capacity, placed in ordinary circumstances. Yet, by extraordinary piety she stands out before all the ages as the model Christian mother.

Hannah was the wife of Elkanah, who

was a person very much like herself—unromantic and plain, never having fought a battle or been the subject of a marvelous escape. Neither of them would have been called a genius. Just what you and I might be—that was Elkanah and Hannah.

The brightest time in all the history of that family was the birth of Samuel. Although no star ran along the heavens pointing down to his birthplace, I think the angels of God stooped at the coming of so wonderful a prophet.

As Samuel had been given in answer to prayer, Elkanah and all his family, save Hannah, started up to Shiloh to offer sacrifices of thanksgiving. The pillow that cradles her infant's head is the altar of the mother's heart. But when the boy was old enough she took him to Shiloh and took three bullocks, an ephah of flour, a bottle of wine and made offering of sacrifice unto the Lord. There, according to a previous vow, she left him, to stay all the days of his life and minister in the temple.

Years rolled on and every year Hannah made with her own hand a garment for Samuel and took it to him. The lad would have gotten along quite well without the garment, for I suppose he was well clad by the ministry of the temple. But Hannah could not be contented unless she was all the time doing something for her darling boy.

"Moreover his mother made him a little coat and brought it to him from year to year, when she came up with her husband to offer the yearly sacrifice."

Hannah stands before you then, in the first place, as an INDUSTRIOUS mother. There was no need for her to work. Elkanah, her husband, was far from poor. He belonged to a distinguished family. The Bible tells us he was the son of Jeroham, the son of Elihu, the son of Tohu, the son of Zuph. "Who were they?" you ask. I do not know. But they were distinguished people, no doubt, or their names would not have been mentioned.

Hannah might have seated herself with her family and, with folded arms and disheveled hair, read novels from year to year—had there been novels to read. But when I see her making that garment and taking it to Samuel, I know she is industrious from principle as well as from pleasure. God would not have a mother become a drudge or a slave. He would have her employ all the helps possible in this day in rearing her children.

But Hannah ought never to be ashamed

to be found making a coat for Samuel!

Most mothers need no counsel in this direction. The wrinkled brow, the pallor of cheek, the thimble-mark on their finger—all attest they are faithful in maternal duties. The bloom, the brightness and vivacity of girlhood have given place for the grander dignity, usefulness and industry of motherhood.

But there is a heathenish idea getting abroad in some of the families of Americans. There are mothers who banish themselves from the home circle.

For three-fourths of their maternal duties they prove themselves incompetent. They are ignorant of what their children wear, what their children eat and what their children need. They intrust to irresponsible persons these young immortals and allow them to be under influences which may cripple their bodies, taint their purity, spoil their manners or destroy their souls.

From the awkward cut of this modern Samuel's coat, you know his mother did not make it. Out from under flaming chandeliers, off from imported carpets and down the granite stairs, there has come a great crowd of children in this day—untrained, saucy, incompetent for all practical duties of life, ready to be caught in the first whirl of crime and sensuality.

Indolent and unfaithful mothers will make indolent and unfaithful children. You cannot expect neatness and order in any house where the daughters see nothing but slatternness and upside-downness in their parents. Let Hannah be idle and most certainly Samuel will grow up idle.

Who are the industrious men in all our occupations and professions? Who are they who are managing the merchandise of the world, building the walls, tinning the roofs, weaving the carpets, making the laws, governing the nations, making the earth to quake, heave, roar and rattle with the tread of gigantic enterprises? Who are they? For the most part they descended from industrious mothers who, in the old homestead, used to spin their own yarn, weave their own carpets, plait their own doormats, cane their own chairs and do their own work while rearing their children.

The stalwart men and the influential women of this day, 99 out of 100 of them, came from such an illustrious society of hard knuckles and homespun.

And who are these people in society,

light as froth, blown by every wind of temptation and fashion—peddlers of filthy stories, dancing-jacks of political parties, the scum of society, tavern-lounging men of low wink and filthy chuckle and rotten associations? For the most part they came from mothers idle and disgusting—the scandalmongers of society, going from house to house attending to everybody's business but their own, believing in witches and ghosts and horseshoes to keep the devil out of the churn—by a godless life setting their children on the very verge of hell.

The mothers of Samuel Johnson, Alfred the Great, Isaac Newton, St. Augustine, Richard Cecil and President Edwards for the most part were industrious and hard-working.

Now, while I congratulate all Christian mothers who have the wealth and modern contrivances which afford them all kinds of help, let me say that every mother ought to be, by the hour, observant of her children's walk, behavior, food, looks and companionships.

The Bible does not speak well of hirelings, at best. Whatever help Hannah may have, I think she ought every year, at least, to make one garment for her Samuel. The Lord have mercy on the man who is so unfortunate as to have had a lazy mother or to have been reared by hirelings.

Again, Hannah stands before you as an INTELLIGENT mother. From the way in which she talked in this Bible chapter and the way she managed this boy, you know she was intelligent. There are no persons in a community who need to be so wise and well-informed as mothers. Alertness is a motherly requirement.

Oh, this work of culturing children for this world and the next! This child is timid and must be roused up and pushed out into activity. Another is forward and must be held back and tamed down into modesty and politeness. Rewards for one, punishments for another. That which will make George will ruin John. The rod is necessary in one case, while a frown of displeasure is more than enough in another—for there have been children who have grown up and gone to glory without ever having had their ears boxed.

Oh, how much care and intelligence are necessary in the rearing of children! But in this day, when there are so many books on the subject, no parent is excusable in being ignorant of the best mode of bringing up a child.

If parents knew more of dietetics there would be fewer dyspeptic stomachs, weak nerves and inactive livers among children. If parents knew more of art and were in sympathy with all that is beautiful, there would not be so many children coming out in the world with boorish proclivities.

If parents knew more of Christ and set adult example, practicing His ways, there would not be so many little feet already starting on the wrong road. All around us voices of riot and blasphemy would not sound with such ecstasy of infernal triumph.

The eaglets in the aerie have no advantages over the eaglets of a thousand years ago. Kids have no superior way of climbing up the rocks than the old goats taught hundreds of years ago. Whelps know no more now than whelps knew ages ago— they are taught no more by the lions of the desert. But it is a shame that in this day, when there are so many opportunities for improving themselves in the best manner of cultivating children, so often there is no more advancement in this respect than there has been among the eaglets, kids and whelps.

Again, Hannah stands before you as a

CHRISTIAN mother. From her prayers and from the way she consecrated her son to God, I know she was good. A mother may have the finest culture, the most brilliant surroundings, but she is not fit for her duties unless she be a Christian mother.

There may be well-read libraries in the home, exquisite music in the parlor, canvas of the best artists on the walls. The children may be wonderful in their attainments and make the house ring with laughter and innocent mirth. But there is something woefully lacking in that house if it is not also the residence of a Christian mother. What wondrous advantages she has in being, herself, a child of God!

I thank God that there are not many prayerless mothers—not many of them. The weight of responsibility is so great they feel a need of a Divine hand to help, a Divine voice to comfort and a Divine heart to sympathize.

Thousands of mothers have been led into the kingdom of God by the hands of their little children. There are hundreds of mothers who would not have been Christians had it not been for the prattle of their little ones. Standing one day in the nursery, they bethought themselves: "This child God has given me to raise for eternity! What is my influence? Not being a Christian myself, how can I expect my child to become a Christian? Lord, help me!"

Are there anxious mothers who know nothing of the infinite spiritual help? Then I commend to them Hannah, the pious mother of Samuel.

Do not think it absolutely impossible that your children come up iniquitous. Out of just such fair brows, bright eyes, soft hands and innocent hearts crime gets its victims. It extirpates purity from the heart, rubs smoothness from the brow, quenches the lustre of the eye—shriveling up, poisoning, putrefying, scathing, scalding, blasting and burning with shame and woe.

Every child is a bundle of tremendous possibilities. Whether that child shall come forth with heart attuned to eternal harmonies and after a life of usefulness on earth go to a life of joy in heaven, or shall jar eternal discords and after a life of wrongdoing on earth shall go to a home of impenetrable darkness in the abyss is being decided by nursery song, Sunday lesson, evening prayer, and walk and look and frown and smile.

Oh, how many children in glory, crowd-

ing all the battlements and lifting a mil-
lion-voiced hosanna, were brought to God
through Christian parentage!

One hundred and twenty clergymen
were together, telling their personal experience and ancestry. How many of them
do you suppose assigned as the means of
their conversion the influence of a Christian mother? One hundred! Philip Doddridge
was brought to God by the Scripture lesson on the Dutch tile of a chimney fire-
place. The mother thinks she is only rocking a child, but she may be rocking the
fate of nations, rocking the glories of
heaven. And you ask why I should in-
clude a discourse on motherhood in my
series on marriage?

Alas, the same maternal power that may
lift a child up may press a child down. A
daughter came to a worldly mother and
said she was anxious about her sins. She
had been praying all night. The mother
said: "Oh, stop praying! I don't believe in
praying. Get over all these religious no-
tions and I'll give you a $500 dress to
wear next week to the party."

The daughter took the dress. She moved
in the party circle that night and set the
pattern to follow. Sure enough, all spiritual impressions were gone. She stopped

praying. A few months later she was on her deathbed. In her closing moments she said: "Mother, I wish you would bring me that $500 dress."

The mother thought it a strange request but brought it to please the dying child. "Now," said the daughter, "Mother, hang that dress on the foot of my bed." The dress was hung. Then the dying girl got up on one elbow, looked at her mother, pointed to the dress and said: "Mother, that dress is the price of my soul."

Oh, what a momentous thing it is to be a mother!

Lastly, Hannah stands before you as the REWARDED mother. For all the coats she made for Samuel, for all the prayers she prayed for him, for the discipline she exerted over him, she got abundant compensation in the piety, usefulness and popularity of her son. That is true in all ages. Every mother gets full pay for all the prayers and tears in behalf of her children.

The progress of the son echoes gladness in the Christian heart that taught him to be earnest and honest. The story of what he does and the influence he exerts goes back to the old homestead—for there is someone always ready to carry good tidings. That story makes the needle in the old mother's tremulous hand fly quicker and the flail in the father's hand come down upon the barn floor with a vigorous thump. Parents love to hear good news from their children!

Look out for the young man who speaks disrespectfully of his father, calling him "the governor," "the squire," or "my old man." Look out for the young woman who calls her mother her "maternal ancestor" or "the old woman."

God grant that all you parents may have the great satisfaction of seeing your children grow up Christians. Oh, the pang of that mother who, after a life of street-gadding and gossip-retailing while hanging on her children the fripperies and follies of this world, sees those children tossed out on the sea of life like foam on the wave—nonentities in a world where only stalwart character can stand the shock. But blessed be the mother who looks upon her children as sons and daughters of the Lord God Almighty!

Oh, the satisfaction of Hannah in seeing Samuel serving at the altar, of Mother Eunice seeing her Timothy learned in the Scriptures. That is the mother's recompense, to see children coming up useful in the world, reclaiming the lost, healing the sick, pitying the ignorant—earnest and useful in every sphere.

That throws a new light back on the old family Bible whenever she reads it. That will be ointment to soothe the aching limbs of decrepitude and light up the closing hours of life's day with the glories of an autumnal sunset!

There she sits—the old Christian mother, ripe for heaven. Her eyesight is almost gone but the splendors of the celestial city kindle up her vision. The brilliance of heaven's morn has struck through the gray locks which are folded back over the winkled temples. She stoops very much now under the burden of care she has carried for her children.

She sits at home, too old to find her way to the house of God. But while she sits there, the past comes back with the children who 40 years ago tripped around her armchair with their griefs and joys and sorrows. Those children are gone now, some caught up into a better realm where they shall never die and others out in the broad world, testing the excellency of a Christian mother's discipline.

Her last days are full of peace. And calmer and sweeter will her spirit become, until the gates of life shall lift and let the worn-out pilgrim into eternal springtide and youth—where the limbs never ache and the eyes never grow dim and the staff of the exhausted and decrepit pilgrim shall become the crown of the victorious immortal athlete.

Mother!

CHAPTER SIX

THE CURSE OF EASY DIVORCE

"Wherefore they are no more twain, but one flesh. What therefore God hath joined together, let not man put asunder" (Matthew 19:6).

IS that blessed text so obscure of meaning and so difficult in interpretation as to permit variance of Christian viewpoint or practice? Is God's will not clearly therein stated?

That there are hundreds and thousands of unhappy homes in America no one will doubt. If there were only one skeleton in the closet, the closet might be locked up and abandoned. But in many a home there is a skeleton in every room and in the hallway.

"Unhappily married"—two words descriptive of many a homestead. It needs no orthodox minister to prove to a badly-mated pair that there is a hell. They are there now!

Sometimes a grand and gracious woman will be thus incarcerated. Her life will be a crucifixion, as was the case with Mrs. Sigourney, the great poetess and great soul. Sometimes a consecrated man will be united to a fury—as was John Wesley, or to a vixen—as was John Milton.

Sometimes, and generally, both parties are to blame. Thomas Carlyle is an intolerable scold and his wife smokes and swears. Froude, the historian, opens the revealing curtain on the lifelong squabble at Craigenputtock and Cheyne Row.

Some say easy divorce is a good prescription for the alleviation of all these domestic disorders of which we hear. But you know and I know that wholesale divorce is one of our national scourges. I am not surprised at this when I think of the influences which have been abroad, militating against the marriage relationship.

For many years the platforms of the country rang with talk about a free-love millennium. There were meetings of this sort held all over the land. Some of the women who were most prominent in that movement have since been distinguished for great promiscuity of affection, thus revealing their basic lack of character and disqualification for representation of womanhood in any case.

Popular themes of such occasions were the tyranny of man, the oppression of the marriage relationship, women's rights and the affinities. Prominent speakers were women with short curls, short dress and very long tongue—everlastingly at war with God because they were created women. On the platform sat meek men with soft accent and cowed demeanor, apologetic for masculinity and holding the parasols while the quarrelsome, scolding orators went on preaching the gospel of free love.

That campaign of about 20 years set more demons into the marriage relationship than will be exorcised in the next 50. Men and women went home from such meetings so permanently confused as to who were their wives and husbands that they never got out of the perplexity. Immeasurable harm was wrought.

Criminal and civil courts tried to disentangle the Iliad of woes and this one got alimony while that one got a limited divorce. This mother kept the children on condition the father could sometimes come look at them. These went into poor-houses and those went into insane asylums. Many went into dissolute public life and all went to destruction.

The mightiest war ever waged against the marriage institution was that free-love campaign right here in America, sometimes under one name and sometimes under another.

Another influence that has warred against marriage in this country has been a festering, pustulous literature—with its millions of sheets every week choked with stories of domestic wrongs, infidelities, massacres and outrages. It is a wonder to me that there are any decencies or any common sense left on the subject of marriage. Half of the news stands of Brooklyn and New York and all our cities reek with the filth.

"Now," say some, "we admit to all these evils and the only way to clear them out and correct them is by easy divorce." Well, before we yield to that cry, let us find out how easy it is now.

I have looked over the laws of all the states and I find that while it is easier in some states than in others, it is easy in every state. Illinois, through its legislature, recites a long list of proper causes for divorce—then closes by giving to the courts the right to make a decree of divorce in any case where they deem it expedient.

After that you are not surprised at the announcement that in one county of Illinois, in one year, there were 833 divorces. If you want to know how easy it is, you have only to look over the records. In the city of San Francisco 333 divorces in 1880, in 20 years in New England, 20,000. Is that not easy enough?

If the same ratio of multiplied divorces and multiplied causes of divorce continues, we are not far from the time when our courts will have to set apart entire days for application. All you will have to prove against a man will be that he left his newspaper or shoes in the middle of the floor. All you will have to prove against a woman will be that she did not immediately sew a button back on her husband's overcoat.

The disease is not rampaging in the United States alone. France and England have also seen divorce doubled in a few years. But to show how very easy divorce is, I have to tell you that in Western Reserve, Ohio, the proportion of divorces to marriages is 1 to 11; in Rhode Island, 1 to

13; in Vermont, 1 to 14. Is not that easy enough?

I want you to notice that frequency of divorce always goes along with the dissoluteness of society. Rome for 500 years had not one case of divorce. Those were her days of glory and virtue. Then the reign of vice began and divorce became epidemic. Rome fell!

What we want in this country and in all lands is that divorce be made more and more and more difficult. Then people, before they enter the relationship, will be persuaded there will probably be no way out of marriage except through the door of the grave. Then they will pause on the verge of marriage until they are fully satisfied it is best, right and happiest.

Then we shall have no more marriage in fun! Frill and flippancy will not prevail. Then men and women will not enter marriage with the idea it is only a trial trip and if they do not like it they can get off at the first convenient landing.

Then this whole question will be taken out of the FRIVOLOUS into the TREMENDOUS and there will be no more joking about the blossoms in a bride's hair than about the flowers on a coffin!

What we want is that the Congress of

the United States at this present session move for changing the national Constitution so a law can be passed which shall be uniform all over the nation. How is it now? If a party to marriage gets dissatisfied, it is only necessary to move to another state to achieve liberation from the domestic tie. Divorce is effected so easily the first party only knows of it by chancing to see it in the newspaper.

There are states which practically put a premium on the disintegration of marriage. Other states (like our own New York State) have the preeminent idiocy of making marriage lawful at 12 and 14 years of age. Thus do we cry out for uniform national control by a good, honest, righteous, comprehensive law that will control everything from Sandy Hook to the Golden Gate.

That will put an end to brokerages in marriage. That will send divorce lawyers into a decent business. That will set people to considering how they can get along together and adjust to more or less unfavorable circumstances rather than seeking to end the relationship and get away from one another.

More difficult divorce will put a stop, to a great extent, upon marriage as a financial speculation. There are men who enter marriage just as they enter the stock market. They find out how much the lady's inheritance might be and that becomes their primary calculation for entering upon the relationship. After all, if it doesn't WORK out they can BACK out! There is total lack of moral principle.

Now, suppose a man understood (as he ought to understand) that if he marries there is no possibility, or extremely low probability, of getting out. What a different perspective. He would be more slow to put his neck in the yoke.

Rigorous divorce law would also help to hinder women from the fatal mistake of marrying men to reform them, as is so alarmingly common!

If a young man has the habit of strong drink fixed on him, he is as certainly bound for a drunkard's grave as that the train starting out from Grand Central Station at eight o'clock tomorrow morning is bound for Albany. The train may not reach Albany, for it may be thrown from the track. The young man may not reach a drunkard's grave, for he may possibly be thrown off the iron track of evil habit. But the probability is high that the train that starts for Albany will get there and the probability is that the young man will arrive at the drunkard's grave.

She who would choose such a man flies in the face of common sense. She knows he drinks, though he tries to hide it by chewing cloves. Everyone knows he drinks. Parents warn, neighbors and friends warn. But she WILL marry him! She WILL reform him!

And if she is unsuccessful in the grand experiment, the divorce law will emancipate her. Habitual drunkenness is a prime cause for divorce in nearly all the states. So the poor thing goes to the altar of sacrifice. If you will show me the poverty-stricken streets in any city I will show you the homes of the women who married men to reform them!

In one case out of 10,000 it may be a successful experiment, but the odds make it the world's worst gamble. Personally, I never saw the successful experiment. But have a rigorous divorce law and that woman will say: "If I marry that man it is for life"—a much-needed deterrent.

A rigorous divorce law will do much to hinder otherwise hasty and inconsiderate marriages. Under the impression that one can be easily released, people marry without inquiry and without reflection. Romance and impulse rule the day.

Perhaps the only ground for the marriage compact is that she likes his looks and he admires the graceful way she passes out the ice cream at the picnic! It is all they know about each other. It is all the preparation for a life together. What tragic superficiality.

A woman who could not make a loaf of bread to save her life and is, herself, undomesticated will swear to "cherish and obey." A Christian will marry an atheist. That always makes combined wretchedness. If a man does not believe there is a God, he is neither to be trusted with a dollar nor with your lifelong happiness.

By the wreck of 10,000 homes by the holocaust of 10,000 sacrificed men and women, by the hearthstone of the family (which is the cornerstone of the state) and in the name of that God who hath made the breaking of the marital oath the most appalling of all perjuries, I implore the Congress of the United States to make some righteous, uniform law for all the states on this subject of marriage and divorce.

Let me say to the hundreds of young people in my audience this morning, before you give your heart and hand in holy alliance—and did you note I said HOLY alliance?—use all caution! Inquire outside as to habits, explore the disposition, scrutinize the taste, question the ancestry, find out the ambitions, look for genuine character.

Do not take the heroes and heroines of cheap novels for a model. Do not put your lifetime happiness in the keeping of a man who has a reputation for being morally questionable or of a woman who dresses carelessly. These blotches are outer signs of inner rot.

Remember that while good looks are a kindly gift of God, wrinkles or accident may despoil them soon enough. Remember that Byron was celebrated as much for his depravity as for his appearance. Remember that your Bible's Absalom had habits more despicable than his hair was splendid.

Hear it! Hear it! The only foundation for happy marriage that ever has been or ever will be is GOOD CHARACTER!

Ask God whom you shall marry, if you marry at all. A union formed in prayer will be a happy union, though sickness pale the cheek, poverty empty the bread tray, death open the small graves and all the path of life be strewn with thorns from the marriage altar with its wedding march and orange blossoms clear on down to the last farewell at the gate where Isaac and Rebecca, Abraham and Sarah, Adam and Eve parted.

Let me say to you who are already in the marriage relationship:

If you make one man or woman happy you have not lived in vain. Christ says that what He is to the Church you ought to be to one another. If sometimes, through difference of opinion or disposition, you make up your mind your marriage was a mistake, patiently bear and forbear. Remember that life at the longest is short and that for those who have been badly mated in this world death will give quick and immediate bill of divorcement, written in letters of green grass on quiet graves.

And perhaps, my brother, my sister, perhaps you may appreciate each other better in heaven than you have on earth. In the "Farm Ballads" our American poet puts into the lips of a repentant husband, after a life of married perturbation, these suggestive words:

*"And when she dies I wish that she
      would be laid by me,
And lying together in silence, perhaps
      we will agree.
And if ever we meet in heaven, I would
      not think it queer
If we love each other better because we
      quarreled here."*

Let me say to you who are in happy married union: avoid first quarrels, have no unexplained correspondence with former admirers, cultivate no suspicions. In a moment of bad temper do not rush out and tell the neighbors. Do not let any of the gadabouts of society unload in your house their baggage of gab and tittle-tattle. Do not stand on your rights. Learn how to apologize. Do not be so proud or so stubborn or so devilish that you will not make up.

The worst domestic misfortunes and the most scandalous divorce cases started from little infelicities. The whole piled-up train of rail cars, telescoped and smashed at the bottom on an embankment and 100 feet down, came to that catastrophe by getting just two or three inches off the track. Some of the greatest domestic misfortunes and the widest-resounding divorce cases have started from little misunderstandings that were allowed to go on and on until home, respectability, religion and immortal soul went down in the crash—CRASH!!!

Fellow citizens as well as fellow Christians—let us have a divine rage against anything that wars against the marriage estate!

Blessed institution! Instead of two arms to fight the battle of life—four! Instead of two eyes to scrutinize the path of life—four! Instead of two shoulders to lift the burden of life—four! Twice the energy, the courage, the holy ambition, the probability of worldly success, twice the prospects of heaven.

Into that matrimonial bower God fetches two souls. Outside the bower is room for all contentions, bickerings and controversies; but inside that bower there is room for only one guest—the angel of love. Let that angel stand at the floral doorway, sword drawn, to hew down the worst foe of that union: easy divorce!

CHAPTER SEVEN

A PLAIN TALK

"Let every one in particular love his own wife even as himself; and the wife see that she reverence her husband" (Ephesians 5:33).

ALL this good advice comes from a man who never married, the Apostle Paul. He lived to nearly 60 years of age in eminent bachelorhood. Indeed, he reminds us it was better for him to remain in single life because he went on such rapid missionary expeditions that no companion could have endured the hardship. Celibacy in some cases is best. Such persons accomplish under such circumstances much which could not be accomplished in the married style of life.

I have known men who remained unwed that they might take care of the children of a deceased brother. And what would become of the world without the self-sacrifice and helpfulness of maiden aunts, I cannot imagine.

Among the brightest queens of heaven will be those who took care of other people's children. Alas for that household that has not, within easy call, an Aunt Mary! I know there are caricatures and ungallant things sometimes said. But so far as my observation goes, they are quite equal in disposition to their married sisters.

While Paul remained in the single state, he kept his eyes open. He looked off upon the calm sea of married life and upon the stormy sea of domestic disorder and confusion. He comes forth in my text to say: "Let every one in particular love his own wife as himself; and the wife see that she reverence her husband"—implying that the wife ought to be lovable so there might be something to love and the man ought to be honorable so there might be something to reverence.

It is a most congratulatory thought that the vast majority of people in the married state are well mated. When the news is first announced to the outside world of the betrothal there may be surprise and seeming incongruity, but as years pass it is demonstrated that the selection was appropriate.

There may be great difference of temperament, great difference of appearance, great difference of circumstances and upbringing. That is no objection. The sanguine and the phlegmatic temperaments make appropriate union—the blonde and the brunette, the quick and the slow, the French and the German. In the machinery of domestic life there is more need for the driving-wheel than for the brakes, but both are essential. The best union, it seems, generally has opposites.

The best argument in behalf of marriage as a Divine institution is the fact that the vast majority of such relationships are the very best thing that could have happened for the parties involved. Once in a while there is a resounding exception to the good rule, as an attempt is made to marry fire and gunpowder— with the consequent explosion. But in the clear majority of instances the relationship is a beautiful illustration of what the Psalmist said when he declared: "God setteth the solitary in families."

Taking it for granted, then, that you are well-mated, I proceed to give you some prescriptions for domestic happiness.

First of all, a spirit of COMPROMISE must be dominant. You must remember that you were 20 or 30 years forming independent habits and having your own way as part of the growing-up and maturing process. In marriage, these habits must be brought into accord. There may be some ingenuity necessary.

Be determined to have your own way and there will be no peace. Let the rule be: In all matters of moral principle your determination shall be rigid as iron and in all unimportant matters pliable as willow.

Whatever you may think of the word "compromise" in politics, without compromise there simply is no domestic peace. A great many people are willing to compromise if you will do just as they want you to do. There is no compromise in that! The rule ought to be: In all domestic, social, ecclesiastical and political matters, firm adherence to fundamentals and easy surrender in nonessentials. Be not too proud or too stubborn to give up. Compromise! Compromise!

Then, there must be a spirit of CONSULTATION. "Talking things over" is part of the relationship.

There is an absurd rule we hear abroad

in the world—that men ought never to take their business home. In the first place, woman has a capacity to judge moral character which man has not. Before you invite into your business partnership any man, you ought to introduce him to your wife and get her judgment as to his capacity and integrity. After five minutes' conversation she will tell you as much about him as you will know at the close of 20 years—and you may find out too late.

A man proposes to come into your business partnership. You take him to your home. He tarries a little while and is gone. You say to your wife: "Well, what do you think of him?" She says: "I don't like him at all." You say: "It's absurd to form a prejudice against him on so short an acquaintance. I have known him for years and have never known any bad against him." "Well," she says, "I don't know why I have formed that opinion, but I tell you to beware. Put none of your financial interests into that man's keeping."

Ten or 15 years pass by. You come home some night and say: "Well, my dear, you were right. That man swindled me out of my last dollar." It is not because she is wiser than you. It is because God has given her that peculiar intuition in regard to human character. It does not explain why, when it comes to matters of the heart, some women make such poor decisions in regard to whom they should marry. That is a different matter, which we have already addressed.

Now, you have no right to go into an enterprise which involves the fate of your entire family without home consultation. Of course, this implies that you did not marry an imbecile. If at the marriage altar you committed suicide, you had better keep all your business affairs in your own heart and head. But let us hope you have sound common sense presiding in your household.

How much a wife may help a husband's business affairs was well illustrated in the case where the wife saved from the family allowance a certain amount of money for the proverbial "rainy day." There was that day when the husband came home and said: "Well, I must suspend payment tomorrow. A few dollars would get me through but I cannot get that few dollars and am going to ruin!"

That evening the wife said: "I wish you would hunt up the definition of the word 'independence' in the dictionary. Please hunt it up for me." He opened the dictionary and found the word. Right opposite it was a $100 bill.

"Now," she said, "I would like to have you find the word 'gratitude.'" He turned to the word—and there was another $100 bill. Before the evening was past she asked him to read a verse of a certain chapter of the Bible. He opened to the verse and there was $500. He now had financial relief to tide him over his disaster.

You call that dramatic? I call that beautifully Christian.

In expenditures there ought to be consultation. Do not dole out money to your wife as though she were a beggar. Let her know how much you have—or how little. Appeal to her intelligent judgment. She will be content and your own disposition will not be irritated. As long as you keep a mystery about your business matters she will wonder why that allowance is so small.

No honorable woman wants to spend more money than can be afforded. Come into consultation with her on this matter. It is a bad sign when a man dare not tell his business transactions to his wife. There is something wrong!

Do you suppose the gigantic forgeries

which have been enacted in this country would have taken place if the wife had been consulted? She would have said: "Stop! Let us live in one room in the poorest house on the poorest street of the poorest town and have nothing to eat but dry bread rather than that you should make yourself guilty before God and the law." In the vast majority of cases where there has been exposure of great frauds, the wife has been the most surprised person in the community.

A banker some time ago misused trust funds. He went from fraud to fraud and from knavery to knavery until it was necessary for him to leave home before daylight. As he looked in on his sleeping children and kissed his wife good-bye he thought it was for the last time. He was brought back, however, by the constables of an outraged law and is now in the penitentiary.

Do you suppose that man, with a good, honest Christian wife, could have gotten into such a mess had he consulted her in regard to her wishes? Consultation is the word—domestic consultation!

Again, for your mutual happiness there must be a spirit of FORBEARANCE. In the weeks, months and years you were courting, only the more genial side of your two natures was observable. Now you are off guard and faults are obvious on both sides. Having discovered one another's imperfections—forbear!

If the one be given to too much precision and the other is disorderly in habits, if one be spendthrift and the other over-saving, if the one be loquacious and the other reticent—forbear! And especially if you both have inflammable tempers. Do not both get mad at once. Take turn about! William Cowper put it well when he said:

> *"The kindest and the happiest pair*
> *Will find occasion to forbear;*
> *And something every day they live*
> *To pity and perhaps forgive."*

Again, I counsel you, for domestic happiness cultivate each other's SPIRITUAL WELFARE. If religious matters are an irritation in the household it is because you do not understand or appreciate proper spiritual stratagem. One or both of you are wrong. There is dire need for submission to the urgings of the Holy Spirit— just as is true at all times in all things. Earnest prayer and consistent individual lives are a must if the Christian ideal for the home is to be realized.

Of course, there are homes represented here in which one of the marriage partners is not a Christian. Paul put it forcefully when he said: "How knowest thou, O wife, whether thou shalt save thy husband? How knowest thou, O man, whether thou shalt save thy wife?" In this very church, how many have been joined together in spiritual union long after they were wed.

When I find a family in which the wife is a Christian and her husband not, I just frankly say to him: "Now come on in. You might just as well try to swim up the Niagara rapids as against the tide of influence with which this church is going to surge you into Christianity. You must come in! You know your wife is right in this matter. She may fall short in some ways and you may lose patience with her—but you know she is better than you are. You know when she dies she will go as straight to heaven as a shot to a target.

"And if today, on the way home, a vehicle should dash down the street and she should fall lifeless (with no opportunity for last words), you might have doubt about what would become of you and the children, but you would have no doubt about her eternal destiny. Somewhere under the flush of her cheek or under the pallor of her brow is the Lord's mark. She is your wife, but she is God's child. You are not jealous of that relationship and secretly you wish that you, yourself, were a son of the Lord Almighty.

"Come—have the matter settled. If I die before you, I will not forget in the next world how you stood together here. But I will anticipate seeing both of you up there. You must come!

"I say it in all Christian love and emphasis, as a brother talks to a brother: You must come! You have been united so long, you cannot afford to have death divorce you. How long it has been since you began the struggle of life together! You have helped each other over the road and all you have done for each other God only knows.

"There have been tedious sicknesses and anxious watching; here and there a grave, short but very deep. Though the blossoms of the marriage day may have scattered and the lips that pronounced you one may have gone into dust, you have through all these years been to each other true as steel. You must come!"

I do not think I ever read anything more beautiful and quaintly poetic than Cotton Mather's description of the departure of

136 / *The Marriage Ring*

his wife to heaven: "The black day arrives. I had never seen so black a day in all the time of my pilgrimage. The desire of my eyes and heart is this day to be taken from me at a stroke. Her death is lingering and painful. All the forenoon of this day she was in the pangs of death and sensible until the last minute or two before her final expiration.

"I cannot remember the discourse that passed between us, only that her devout soul was full of satisfaction about going to a state of blessedness with the Lord Jesus Christ. As far as my distress would permit, I studied to confirm her satisfaction and consolation.

"When I saw to what a point of resignation I was called of the Lord, I resolved (with His help) to glorify Him. So, two hours before she expired, I knelt by her bedside, took into my hands that dear hand—the dearest in all the world—and solemnly and sincerely gave her up to the Lord. I gently put her out of my hands and laid away her hand, resolved I would not touch it again.

"She afterward told me she signed and sealed my act of resignation, and though before that she had called for me continually she never asked for me any more."

Now, let us be truly faithful in this marriage relationship of which I have been speaking. Do you want to know what the Lord thinks of it? Read the sixty-second chapter of Isaiah, where He says: "As the bridegroom rejoiceth over the bride, so shall thy God rejoice over thee." There is a wedding coming that will eclipse all the princely and imperial weddings the world ever saw!

It was a great day when Napoleon took Josephine; it was a great day when Henry VIII led Anne Boleyn over the cloth of gold on the street which led up to the palace; it was a great day when the King of Spain took Mercedes—but there will be an infinitely, infinitely greater time when the Lord shall take His bride, the Church, to Himself.

Long ago they were betrothed, Christ and His bride, but she has been down in this wilderness. He has written her again and again. The marriage day is fixed. She has sent word to Him. He has sent word to her.

But, oh, was there ever such a difference in estate? The King on the one side—the bride of the wilderness, poor and persecuted, on the other. The wealth of the universe on the one side, the obscurity of the ages on the other. The pomp of heaven on the one side, the poverty of earth on the other. But He will endow her with all His immeasurable wealth and raise her to sit with Him on a throne forever.

Come, thou bridal morn of the ages! Come! There shall be the rumbling of great chariot wheels down the sky. There shall be riders ahead and mounted cavalry behind—the conquerors of heaven on white horses!

Clear the way!

Then the charioteers shall rein in their bounding steeds of fire and the King shall dismount from the chariot. He shall take by the hand the bride of the wilderness with all the crowded galleries of the universe as spectators. Ring all the wedding bells of heaven! The King lifts the bride into the chariot and cries: "Drive on! Drive UP!"

The clouds shall spread their cloth of gold for the procession. The twain shall go through the gates triumphant, up the streets, then step into the palace at the banquet. Ten thousand potentates and principalities and dominations, cherubic and archangelic, with ten thousand gleaming and uplifted chalices, shall celebrate the once-in-eternity day when the

King of heaven and earth brings home His bride from the wilderness.

Make haste, my beloved! Be thou like a roe or a young hart upon the mountains of spices. Make haste!